THE REVISED VERSION
EDITED FOR THE USE OF SCHOOLS

THE REVELATION

OF

St JOHN THE DIVINE

T0381544

THE REVELATION

OF

St JOHN THE DIVINE

EDITED BY

G. H. S. WALPOLE

BISHOP OF EDINBURGH

CAMBRIDGE

AT THE UNIVERSITY PRESS

1911

CAMBRIDGE
UNIVERSITY PRESS

32 Avenue of the Americas, New York NY 10013-2473, USA

Cambridge University Press is part of the University of Cambridge.

It furthers the University's mission by disseminating knowledge in the pursuit of
education, learning and research at the highest international levels of excellence.

www.cambridge.org
Information on this title: www.cambridge.org/9781107458710

© Cambridge University Press 1911

First published 1911
First paperback edition 2014

A catalogue record for this publication is available from the British Library

ISBN 978-1-107-45871-0 Paperback

PREFACE BY THE GENERAL EDITOR
FOR THE NEW TESTAMENT

THE Revised Version has to some extent super-
seded the need of annotation on the books of
the New Testament, so far as the meaning of words
and phrases is concerned. But the present Edition
will, it is hoped, serve a good purpose in drawing the
attention of young scholars to the importance of some
of the changes made in that Version.

Another aim is to present in a clear and intelligible
form the best and most approved results of recent
theological work on these books.

The General Editor takes this opportunity of noting
that, as in *The Cambridge Bible for Schools*, each writer
is responsible for the interpretation of particular pas-
sages, or for the opinion expressed on any point of
doctrine. His own part is that of careful supervision
and occasional suggestion.

ARTHUR CARR.

CONTENTS.

INTRODUCTION

(1) THE APOCALYPSE AND ITS CHARACTER.

Every reader will recognize the very different character
the last book of the New Testament has from all its
predecessors. It is more like the books of Daniel and
Ezekiel, full of visions and strange portents. And it has
a different name, it is not a Gospel or Epistle but a
Revelation, which means an unveiling of the unseen.
But though this kind of writing is unfamiliar to us, it was
not so to those who lived in the first century of our
present era. The book of Enoch, which is full of accounts
of angels and spirits and of the mysteries of the unseen
world, and has many resemblances to the Apocalypse, was
written at different times between B.C. 100 and A.D. 30 and
probably widely read. And this was followed by "the
Book of the Secrets of Enoch," which belongs to the first
half of the first century, and in it are wonderful pictures
of a great sea in the heavens, of a beautiful park full
of fruit trees bearing all kinds of fruits, of great angels
with six wings. A little later there appeared the Revelation of Baruch, who writes to comfort his Jewish brethren
now that the holy city and temple are no more. He bids
them look forward to the coming reign of the Messiah
when a new Jerusalem will be built and Rome the city of
evil will be destroyed. Still later at the end of the first
century after Christ another Apocalypse was issued, called
the Fourth Book of Esdras. It is supposed to contain the

seven visions of Ezra, some of which picture the coming of the Messiah and the destruction of Rome. There are many other writings of the kind, such as the Jewish Sibylline Oracles, which express the same desire to penetrate the veil and to find from visions some interpretations of the strange historic events of the time. And as will have been noticed in this cursory sketch, they have many points of resemblance with the Christian Apocalypse. And not only in figure but also in purpose. Like the book of Daniel, which was probably written in the time of the persecution of Antiochus Epiphanes (B.C. $\frac{168}{165}$) to strengthen the faithful Jews when an attempt was being made to destroy their faith, so these Apocalypses were generally intended to cheer and uplift the spirits of devout Jews when their very existence seemed to be threatened. Now as all this was an expression of the religious spirit of the Apostolic age, what more natural than that it should find a place in the Christian Church? There was sore need of comfort. The Church of the first century passed through a terrible time. Probably none of its leaders escaped persecution and most of them suffered a cruel death at the hands of their enemies. Though Rome was naturally disposed to give a licence to the various religions of the subjected nations, was not disposed for example to find fault with the worship of Ephesus; the Christian religion was not national, it did not belong to one people or tribe more than another. It had a universal mission and as such was an element of disturbance in every religion. It would leave nothing alone, but claimed disciples from the Roman, Ephesian, Egyptian, Asiatic faiths alike. It was therefore bound to be persecuted. And our Lord had prepared His disciples for it. He had told them what to do and how to behave. But in spite of His warnings, persecution when it came was hard to face. Homes were destroyed, parents robbed of their children, and husbands of their wives, Christians boycotted, worship proscribed

and every kind of contempt shewn to a religion that seemed
weak and defenceless. The Christians who believed in
the all-conquering might of their unseen Leader and the
possibility of His immediate return were often much per-
plexed. And the Neronian persecution with its brutal
cruelty made the truth of the Kingdom of Christ still more
difficult to receive. Further, this special trial was not made
more easy by the wars, earthquakes, and volcanic erup-
tions which were characteristic of that first age. Questions
were asked as to Divine Government which could not
be satisfactorily answered or put aside. It was not
unnatural therefore that the help which God sent should
take the shape of an Apocalypse or Revelation, for it was
in this way that He had helped the Jewish Church in
similar difficulties. The immediate object and purpose
of the book therefore is not to give, as has been sometimes
thought, a prophecy of all future history, the wickedness
of the Papacy, the ambition of Napoleon or the rise of
some great social revolution, but to shew the Christians
of that first century what the book of Daniel had shewn
the Jews some three hundred years before, how that all
these things were foreseen by God and, horrible though
they were, allowed to have a place in His plan. The
book when looked at in this light is not so difficult to
understand as might be supposed. And if it helps us,
as it certainly does, to read the message of that stormy
time, it will help us to understand the mystery of every
like age and so comes to be of eternal value.

(2) THE STRUCTURE.

The book is divided into two almost equal portions,
each so complete in itself, that they might be regarded as
separate volumes. They are alike in this that they shew
that Christ the King not only knows the evil His children
are enduring, but by His wisdom uses it to bring about

a greater good. The first volume is concerned with Christ's relation to the Church and the world in general, the second, His special relation to the hostile powers that are trying to destroy her.

VOL. I (Chapters i—xi). First, we have a picture of the actual Church as represented in the seven Churches of Asia and only two are seen to be free from rebuke. The Church therefore is in need of purification. She cannot do without adversity and trial. This is succeeded by a vision of the Glory of God, of His Holiness and Majesty, and of the mystery that enwraps His plans which no one has yet been able to penetrate. It was the meaning of the Divine Providence that the Seer expected to see, and he is much disappointed when it seems to him at first that the secret will never be divulged. At last, to his joy, He sees the Christ come forward to open the book and to unfold the mysteries contained in it. The remainder of the volume describes what he sees, how earthquakes, wars, catastrophes, persecutions are really steps in the progress of human society ; either removing obstacles, as the breaking of a seal enables one to get at a letter, or trumpet calls, i.e. stern appeals to the deaf conscience of the wicked to give up its rebellion. But though so painful to the world, the Church is seen to be quite safe and even to thrive under these terrible judgments.

VOL. II. The second volume (xii—xxii) shews us the Church, out of which has sprung the Incarnate Christ, under the figure of a woman arrayed with the sun, persecuted by the Dragon who uses both the civil and religious powers of the world to crush it. Rome and Paganism alike inspired by his fiendish hatred do their best but fail. This is the very heart of the mystery which so far has not yet been explained. And it is against these enemies that the Kingdom of God wars with its terrible judgments. At last, though we are not told when, Rome, Paganism, and the Dragon are over-

thrown. It is in this part of the book that the chief
difficulty is found, as it was necessary for the safety of the
Christians that the message should be expressed in such
dark figures that if copies were discovered they should
not lead to any being implicated. So Rome is disguised
as Babylon, Nero as the beast with the number 666, and
the other emperors in other veiled language. The ultimate
triumph and glory of the persecuted Church is shewn under
the mysterious symbolism of the heavenly city.

(3) THE AUTHOR.

The writer speaks of himself both at the end and the
beginning of the book as John, but there is no further
description designating what John is meant[1]. It would
be natural to suppose that one who writes thus simply
would be the Apostle, as being the most prominent person
in the Church of that name. And this was the earliest
belief. Justin who lived at Ephesus before he went to
Rome, about the year 135, speaks of the Apocalypse as
the work of the Apostle, and Irenæus, who wrote about
A.D. 180, gives a common authorship to the Gospel and
Apocalypse, both as being written by John the disciple of
the Lord[2]. With this other early writers agree and the first
suggestion that some other John wrote it comes nearly a
hundred years later from Dionysius, a Bishop of Alexandria,
who on the grounds of the difference of thought, style and
language concludes that the Author of the Apocalypse
must not be identified with the Author of the Gospel.
The chief difficulty he feels to lie in the language. "The
Gospel and first Epistle are written in correct and flowing
Greek and there is not a barbarism, solecism or provincial-
ism in them : whereas the Greek of the Apocalypse is
inaccurate, disfigured by unusual or foreign words and
even at times solecistic." This argument against the

[1] i. 1, 4, 9 ; xxii. 8.
[2] See Swete's Introduction, p. ciii. and foll.

Johannine authorship is weighty but not overwhelming. Had Greek been the Apostle's native language it would have been impossible to suppose that both books came directly or indirectly from the same hand. But we know too little of St John's knowledge of Greek to be sure that he would himself write both books. It is possible that the Apocalypse is his own Greek and the Gospel the Greek of another. It would not be so likely that he would dictate the former as the latter and "early tradition explicitly states that the Gospel was written from dictation and underwent some kind of revision at the hands of those who received it." (Swete, p. clxxix.)

The difference of thought, with the absence of some of the characteristic phrases of the Gospel, is amply explained by the unusual character of the Apocalypse. Such visions as fill the book shew a very marked elevation of spirit such as we call ecstasy, and we should not expect one who was struggling with the limitations of language, to express the large and tumultuous thoughts, surging up under deep spiritual excitement, to use the same images as those natural for a biography. But whilst noting the differences we must not forget "the marked affinities of the two books and the characteristic phrases and ideas which they have in common." These are almost as remarkable as the contrasts and seem to point to a common authorship.

If it be asked whether the Apostle was likely to see such visions and record them, it may be said that of all the Apostles, this quiet meditative spirit, who was constantly contemplating the life of "the Word made flesh" and who had beneath that outward calm, a strong fervent glowing spirit, which won for him the name of Boanerges, was the most likely. Living as tradition asserts to a great age and bearing the trials and sorrows of hundreds of Christians, who were continually telling him of the cruel persecutions and the terrible tribulations through which they had passed ; and having himself borne suffering and exile as a witness to the faith, he would long to find some word of comfort, and in the visions God gave him in Patmos he found it.   It may be asked whether there is any evidence to connect the Apostle with Asia.   Dr Swete sums it up in these words : " The witness of Irenæus shews beyond a doubt that a John who had been a disciple of the Lord resided in Asia within the lifetime of Polycarp, Bishop of Smyrna, who was born (Harnack) in A.D. 69.   A Bishop of Ephesus at the end of the second century asserts that the John who lay on the Lord's breast was buried at Ephesus : and another Asian writer of the same period speaks of a miracle which John the author of the Apocalypse performed in that city " (Swete, p. clxxiv).   And Clement of Alexandria, followed by Origen, speaks of his exile at Patmos.   Such evidence is not absolutely conclusive, but it does not seem likely that Irenæus should have noted the fact of any other John being at Ephesus save the Apostle.   And the more simple the designation, the more likely it seems that the son of Zebedee should be meant.

(4)   THE DATE.

Here tradition is " practically unanimous " in its belief that the Apocalypse was written in the last years of Domitian and with this agree best the thoughts suggested by the book itself.   The condition of the seven Churches gives evidence of a state of things considerably later than anything we read of in the Acts or indeed in the Epistles. Heresies seem in some places to be firmly rooted, definite persecution is treated as history.   And, in the later chapters, the worship of the Cæsars is marked as being clearly pressed, those who refuse being boycotted.   The political condition of affairs in Domitian's reign would suit this. Again, the strange legend of Nero's reappearance after

death which St John makes use of to indicate Domitian—
this being the easiest way of suggesting to those for whom
he writes to whom he refers—cannot very well be applied
to anyone else. If the Apocalypse were written earlier it
is difficult to see to what the mysterious references in
chapters xiii and xvii really refer. But the difficult
passage xvii. 10, 11, 12 suggests that there were two
editions of the Apocalypse, one earlier in Vespasian's
reign, the other in Domitian's.

If early tradition is correct, then the Apocalypse was
written a quarter of a century later than the destruction
of Jerusalem. Chapter xi presents no real difficulties, for
the Temple is only there used as a parable of the Church,
the court indicating mere nominal adherents. We may
therefore conclude that the book was written, or the
second edition of it sent forth, in the last years of
Domitian (90—96). Dr Swete sums up a very able
discussion with the words: "This date appears to be
consistent with the general character and purpose of the
book. The Apocalypse as a whole presupposes a period
when in Asia at least the Church was compelled to choose
between Christ and Cæsar. And the prophet foresees
that this is no local or passing storm, but one which will
spread over the whole empire and run a long course
ending only with the fall of Paganism and of Rome.
The Coming of the Lord is no longer connected with the
Fall of Jerusalem which is viewed as an event of past
history. A new Jerusalem has taken the place of the old
city of God and the Apocalyptist can already see its ideal
glories revealed." (Swete, *The Apocalypse of St John*, p. c.)

(5) To whom Written.

The Apocalypse is an expansion of the seven letters
to the seven Churches of Asia. Though other Churches
were more important than some of those to whom this
prophecy was addressed, yet these seven cities stood on

the great circular road that bound together the most populous, wealthy and influential part of the province, the West central region[1], and were therefore a very good distributing centre for the message which the Apostle was really addressing to the Church at large. There is no hint anywhere that it was to be confined to Asia. There was need everywhere for some inspired interpretation of the strange and awful perplexities which persecution, famine, fire and sword were continually raising in men's minds. And it was this the Apocalypse gave. No one could read it or hear it read without feeling strengthened and encouraged in the fight that each had to make with cowardice and the awful temptation to apostasy in the easy worship of the Cæsar. "Of the immediate effect of the Apocalypse upon the Asian Churches we cannot judge; certainly they weathered the storm, for in the next Christian writing which comes to us from Asia, the Letters of Ignatius, they are represented as large and flourishing communities. The storm itself passed within two or three years after the date which Irenæus assigns to the Apocalypse: Domitian was assassinated Sept. 18, 96, and the accession of Nerva probably gave peace to the Asian Churches." (Swete, p. xciii.)

(6) THE ANALYSIS.

BOOK I. CHAPTERS I–XI.

Part I. Christ seen in relation to His Church.

i–iii. As King-Priest He rules, warns and encourages the Churches that make up His Body.

Part II. Christ seen in relation to the world.

iv. The Glory of God.

v. The Glory of Christ in God.

---

[1] Ramsay, *Letters to the Seven Churches*, p. 183.

Part III. Christ is seen developing God's plan.

 vi. Christ opens the seals. Consequences to the world.

Part IV. Interlude. Christ is seen protecting the Church from the judgments that fall on the world.

 vii. The sealing of the servants of God.

Part V. Christ is seen summoning the world to surrender.

 viii–ix. The seven trumpet calls of God.

Part VI. Interlude. Christ again assures the Church of His protection.

 x. The end is in sight. "Time shall be no longer."

 xi. 1–13. The true Israel is preserved, the old apostate Israel trodden under foot.

Part VII. Christ is seen triumphing.

 xi. 15–19. The final victory of God's saints.

BOOK II. CHAPTERS XII–XXII.

Part I. Revelation of the mystery of wickedness that lies hidden behind the opposition of the world.

 xii. The birth of Christ and the fury it excites in the great red Dragon.

Part II. The part Rome plays in the spiritual conflict of the Church and the Dragon.

 xiii. The Dragon summons to his aid the Imperial and Provincial powers of Rome. The secret revealed.

Part III. As in the first book so here the Church is assured of her safety.

 xiv–xv. The redeemed are seen enjoying great happiness, the apostates on the other hand are in torment.

Part IV. The Roman Empire is punished for its rebellion against God.

   xvi. The revelation of the vials of the wrath of
   God.

Part V. Rome is judged.

   xvii–xviii. At first Rome seems triumphant, but
   her wickedness and internal dissensions bring
   her to ruin.

   xix. 1–10. The fall of Rome excites great joy in
   the spiritual world.

Part VI. Paganism is judged.

   xix. 11–21. The spiritual conflict with Paganism
   and its complete overthrow.

Part VII. The Dragon is judged.

   xx. Satan is bound and cast into the lake of fire.

Part VIII. Revelation of the City of God.

   xxi. 1–9. The new heaven and new earth with
   a picture of the new society.

   xxi. 9–xxii. 6. The glories of the New Jerusalem.

Part IX. The Epilogue.

   xxii. 6–20. The last words.

(7) BOOKS FOR FURTHER STUDY.

As very different views are taken of the meaning of the
Book of Revelation it is not easy to recommend any
particular commentary, beyond that which has in the
main been followed in these short notes, namely *The
Apocalypse of St John* by Dr H. B. Swete, Regius
Professor of Divinity in the University of Cambridge.
This, which was published in 1906, is not only the latest
study of any importance, but is marked by that rare
scholarship and spiritual wisdom which make Dr Swete

such a fitting successor to the great Cambridge commentators Drs Hort, Lightfoot and Westcott. The Bishop of Ripon's notes in the *Speaker's Commentary* are, as we might expect, marked by much spiritual insight and beauty of expression, and Dr Milligan's notes in the *Expositor's Bible* are of course of much value, but neither of these takes what may be called the historical view and their interpretations therefore differ from those given here. Archbishop Benson's Commentary is of extraordinary interest, but ought to be read from cover to cover rather than consulted for individual interpretations.

THE REVELATION

OF

St JOHN THE DIVINE

BOOK I. CHAPTERS I.—XI.

This first volume treats of the relation of Christ to the Church
and the world. He judges the Church and controls and
orders the destinies of the world. The sorrows and afflic-
tions of the world are seen to be the means of its education.
The Church shares in these, but remains unhurt.

PART I. CHRIST SEEN IN RELATION TO HIS CHURCH.

I.–III. *As King-Priest He rules, warns and encourages
the Churches that make up His Body.*

In the first three chapters we have a Vision of Christ walking in
the midst of the Seven Churches, rebuking, encouraging and
blessing. As Head of the Church, His Body, He speaks
with full authority. The Seven Churches symbolize the
Church Universal, and His relation to them is no more
intimate than that which He bears to the whole Church to-day.

I. 1-3. *Character of the Revelation.*

THE Revelation of Jesus Christ, which God gave him 1
to shew unto his servants, *even* the things which
must shortly come to pass: and he sent and signified *it* by
his angel unto his servant John ; who bare witness of the 2

I. 1. **The Revelation of Jesus Christ, which God gave.** It is
not described as an unveiling of Jesus Christ, but as a Revelation
belonging to Jesus Christ, a Revelation of something in the near
future which the Father shewed to the Son. Nothing can come
to us directly but all through Jesus Christ. It surprises us to
learn that it concerns the near future because in it is revealed the
Fall of Rome and the end of all things, but time has not the
same significance with God as it has with us, with Him a
thousand years are as one day.

unto his servant John. This Revelation Jesus Christ gave to
His servant John in a vision, through spiritual sight rather
than through the reasoning of the mind. The particular John
is simply described as one who had borne witness to the Faith.

word of God, and of the testimony of Jesus Christ, *even*
3 of all things that he saw. Blessed is he that readeth,
and they that hear the words of the prophecy, and keep
the things which are written therein : for the time is at
hand.

4-8. *The writer's greeting to the Churches.*

4 JOHN to the seven churches which are in Asia : Grace
to you and peace, from him which is and which was and
which is to come ; and from the seven Spirits which are
5 before his throne ; and from Jesus Christ, *who is* the
faithful witness, the firstborn of the dead, and the ruler of
the kings of the earth. Unto him that loveth us, and

---

3. Blessed is he that readeth. The Vision is not for the few
but all. The author assumes that it will be read in the congre-
gation and has no doubt that, owing to the nearness of Christ's
coming, the reader and earnest hearer will receive much blessing
through it.

4. John to the seven churches. It seems unlikely that any
other than the Apostle should describe himself simply as John.
Any other but he would naturally, out of modesty, add some
epithet to prevent any one supposing that he was the Apostle.

Note the Apocalypse is a letter, like the Epistle to the
Romans ; it begins with a salutation and ends with a benediction
(xxii. 21). It is a circular letter written to seven churches, not
one. The symbolical use of numbers leads us to believe that
St John saw in these churches a picture typical of the whole
Church. In this sense it would be Catholic in the widest meaning of the word. For "Asia," see Introduction.

from him which is. The greeting is from the Blessed Three
in One. Note the *Father* is described as "the coming one,"
each revelation brings Him nearer ; the Holy Spirit as "the
seven Spirits before the throne," referring to the fulness of
life He brings ; Jesus Christ as the faithful Martyr, the first to
break the bands of death and the rule of kings. Eternity, Life,
Relation to Humanity are the distinguishing characteristics of
the Eternal One.

5. Unto him that loveth us. Greeting is followed by
Doxology.

The writer at the thought of the God from Whom he sends
greeting prostrates himself in lowly adoration, specially bow-
ing before that One Whom he had known so intimately. Christ
is described as the One Who loves, looses and honours. **Note**

loosed us from our sins by his blood ; and he made us *to* 6
be a kingdom, *to be* priests unto his God and Father ; to
him *be* the glory and the dominion for ever and ever.
Amen. Behold, he cometh with the clouds ; and every 7
eye shall see him, and they which pierced him ; and all
the tribes of the earth shall mourn over him. Even so,
Amen.

I am the Alpha and the Omega, saith the Lord God, 8
which is and which was and which is to come, the
Almighty.

9-11. *Occasion of the Vision.*

I John, your brother and partaker with you in the 9
tribulation and kingdom and patience *which are* in Jesus,

---

the better reading "loosed"—not "*washed*." Sin here conceived
as a bondage, a bad habit from which Christ by His Death
freed us. We are now as members of His Church welded into
a kingdom through which He works upon the world. This not
to be identified with the kingdom of God infinitely older and
vaster—of which it is an expression. Note the priestly side of
the kingdom is mentioned, its prayers and intercessions are of
great power.

7. Behold, he cometh. This is the dominant note. See
vv. 1 and 3 and note that Daniel and Zechariah, both apocalyptic
books, are in his mind. He quotes Dan. vii. 13 and Zech. xii. 10.
Christ's coming will bring sorrow as well as joy. No sadness so
bitter as that of realizing a rejected Love.

8. I am the Alpha. These are the words descriptive of
the Father. In xxi. 6 and xxii. 13 they are ascribed to Christ
and indicate the conception St John had of One on Whose
Bosom he reclined so familiarly at the Last Supper.

9. your brother. Though the Apocalypse is a letter, it is
not a letter of the same kind as the three letters we know as
written by St John. The letters to the seven churches are
definite messages from Christ Himself and the rest of the book
is the record of an Apocalypse. This may be the reason why
St John describes himself here simply as " your brother and
companion in tribulation " instead of "elder " as in his second
and third Epistles. It was not the kind of book in which it was
necessary to assert his official position and it was always easier
for him not to do it.

partaker with you in the tribulation and kingdom. Tribulation and patience are kindred thoughts with kingdom which is

was in the isle that is called Patmos, for the word of God
10 and the testimony of Jesus. I was in the Spirit on the
Lord's day, and I heard behind me a great voice, as of a
11 trumpet saying, What thou seest, write in a book, and
send *it* to the seven churches; unto Ephesus, and unto
Smyrna, and unto Pergamum, and unto Thyatira, and
unto Sardis, and unto Philadelphia, and unto Laodicea.

12–20. *The Vision of Christ.*

This, like other Visions of the book, can only be partially por-
trayed. St John is always more intent on the spiritual
meaning than on the artistic presentation. A portrait of
what is described here would be impossible. The meaning
however is clear. Christ is seen in the midst of the seven
churches, in human form, robed as a Priest with the golden
girdle that symbolized Royalty. "His head and His hair
were white like wool," indicating His Eternity : " His eyes
as a flame of fire," shewing the intensity of His gaze: "His
feet like burnished brass," proving His strength : His voice
had that beautiful sound which belongs to falling waters.

12 And I turned to see the voice which spake with me.

---

a spiritual conception meaning the spiritual realm of God as
expressed in the Church of Christ.

Patmos, a rocky and bare island with good anchorage and
"the first or last stopping place for the traveller on his way from
Ephesus to Rome, or from Rome to Ephesus." St John was there
as an exile banished from Ephesus because of his Christian faith,
his devotion to the word of God and his bold witness to Christ.

10. I was in the Spirit, i.e. "I was carried out of myself
(see Acts xii. 11) into a realization of the spirit world, on the
Sunday, the Lord's Day." The Sunday was the Lord's Day
because it commemorated the Lord's Resurrection. It is interesting to note that this wonderful revelation was made to one
who was alone, probably feeling depressed at being cut off from
the weekly Breaking of the Bread and the joyful Services of the
Church.

as of a trumpet. See Exod. xix. 16 where the Divine
Voice is thus described. Here probably it is not the voice of
Christ (see *v.* 15) but of one of His angels.

11. What thou seest. Not what thou hearest, the book
records a Vision, an Unveiling or Revelation.

to the seven churches. These churches were close to one
another, in a circuit of some 500 miles. They were representa-
tive of the whole Church and the message is therefore universal.

And having turned I saw seven golden candlesticks ; and in the midst of the candlesticks one like unto a son 13 of man, clothed with a garment down to the foot, and girt about at the breasts with a golden girdle. And his 14 head and his hair were white as white wool, *white* as snow ; and his eyes were as a flame of fire ; and his feet 15 like unto burnished brass, as if it had been refined in a furnace ; and his voice as the voice of many waters. And he had in his right hand seven stars : and out of 16 his mouth proceeded a sharp two-edged sword : and his countenance was as the sun shineth in his strength. And when I saw him, I fell at his feet as one dead. And 17 he laid his right hand upon me, saying, Fear not ; I am the first and the last, and the Living one ; and I was 18 dead, and behold, I am alive for evermore, and I have the keys of death and of Hades. Write therefore the 19 things which thou sawest, and the things which are, and the things which shall come to pass hereafter ; the 20 mystery of the seven stars which thou sawest in my right hand, and the seven golden candlesticks. The seven

---

17. I fell...as one dead. He who had leaned on His Breast at supper is now struck with such awe that for the moment he loses consciousness. Christ's touch revives and cheers him.

19. Write therefore the things which thou sawest. These words are important as describing not only the speaker but still more the character of the Book of Revelation—it is an unveiling of the present state of the Church and the world and also of the future—it also explains God's secret about the Church. Mystery here does not mean that which is strange and mysterious but a meaning hidden once and now revealed.

20. The seven stars are the angels. The angels are either (1) the Bishops of the churches, or (2) "messengers," perhaps delegates from the churches to the Apostle and addressed as representing the churches, or (3) angels in the usual scriptural sense, spiritual beings, this being the meaning of the word in at least sixty occasions on which it is used in this book. As it is probable from Matt. xviii. 10 that everyone has a guardian angel, so it may be that nations and churches have their

stars are the angels of the seven churches: and the
seven candlesticks are seven churches.

II. 1-7. *Letter to the Church in Ephesus.*

Ephesus was a city of great importance, commercially and
religiously. All the Eastern trade found a natural opening
to the sea at Ephesus, for at that time the silting up of
the mouth of the river Cayster had been stopped. The
streets were full of merchants, traders and workmen. A
great business was done in St Paul's day in silver shrines,
for Ephesus was the Warden of the Temple of Artemis
(or Diana), one of the wonders of the world. St Paul had
visited it more than once, staying the second time about two
years and evangelizing not only the city but the neighbour-
hood around. At that time the Christian converts had shewn
great devotion and love, sacrificing their magical books and
manifesting to the Apostle, when he left them, warm-
hearted affection. (See Acts xx. 36 and xix. 19.) But in
the course of time, this love had grown cold and the Great
High Priest now warns them that no amount of work,
no zeal for truth will avail unless they regain their early
enthusiasm. This is essential if they would retain their
high position as the leading Church in Asia.

2 To the angel of the church in Ephesus write ;

These things saith he that holdeth the seven stars in
his right hand, he that walketh in the midst of the seven
2 golden candlesticks : I know thy works, and thy toil and
patience, and that thou canst not bear evil men, and

---

representatives in the spiritual sphere. Angels are here taken
as representing the Church. See Dan. x. 20.

the seven candlesticks are seven churches. As the spiritual
side of the churches is represented by a star shining in the
heavens, so its earthly side by a lampstand which holds the light.

II. 1. These things saith he. The description of our Lord in
each case suits the particular Church He addresses. Here He is
seen "walking in the midst of the seven golden candlesticks,"
i.e. moving in and out of the churches and noting their
characteristics. These He has in His own Hand, able to dis-
tinguish them with the same care that a scientific investigator
shews with something he has picked up for careful examination.

2. I know thy works. Christ first mentions the subjects
for praise, the toil—patience—intolerance of evil—wearisome
labours that the Church had cheerfully shewn.

didst try them which call themselves apostles, and they are not, and didst find them false; and thou hast 3 patience and didst bear for my name's sake, and hast not grown weary. But I have *this* against thee, that thou 4 didst leave thy first love. Remember therefore from 5 whence thou art fallen, and repent, and do the first works; or else I come to thee, and will move thy candlestick out of its place, except thou repent. But 6 this thou hast, that thou hatest the works of the Nicolaitans, which I also hate. He that hath an ear, let him 7 hear what the Spirit saith to the churches. To him that overcometh, to him will I give to eat of the tree of life, which is in the Paradise of God.

8–11. *Letter to the Church in Smyrna.*

Smyrna, about 35 miles from Ephesus, was a very fine town with a flourishing trade. The Church was poor and persecuted and this message was sent to cheer and encourage, for a worse trouble was in store than any they had known. Imprisonment and possibly death would have to be faced.

And to the angel of the church in Smyrna write;   8

---

4. I have this against thee. The one drawback, lack of warm affection, was fatal. To fall from love was to fall low. To give up those "first works" which had shewn such affection was to give up power. Love is the secret of influence, and if the Church in Ephesus did not recover it, she would shrink into nothingness. Comp. Matt. xxiv. 12.

6. thou hatest the works of the Nicolaitans. See *vv.* 14 and 20. It is not certain what particular doctrines these people professed or why they were so called. In Acts vi. 5 one of the deacons is called Nicolas a proselyte of Antioch, and Irenæus, an early Christian writer, thinks he originated the sect, but of this there is no proof. It seems quite clear that they had immoral tendencies and taught that so long as a man believed, it did not much matter what his morals were.

7. will I give to eat of the tree of life. From xxii. 2 we learn that the leaves of this tree were for the healing of the nations and from Gen. ii. 9 it would seem that it conferred immortality. Two blessings then are received by those who eat it: (1) that they are healed from any moral disorder to which they may be subject, (2) that they live for ever.

These things saith the first and the last, which was
9 dead, and lived *again*: I know thy tribulation, and thy
poverty (but thou art rich), and the blasphemy of them
which say they are Jews, and they are not, but are a
10 synagogue of Satan. Fear not the things which thou art
about to suffer: behold, the devil is about to cast some
of you into prison, that ye may be tried; and ye shall
have tribulation ten days. Be thou faithful unto death,
11 and I will give thee the crown of life. He that hath an
ear, let him hear what the Spirit saith to the churches.
He that overcometh shall not be hurt of the second
death.

12-17. *Letter to the Church in Pergamum.*

Pergamum was another great city and once superior to Ephesus.
Even now "it was richer in temples and cults than Ephesus"
and a strong centre of paganism—"a throne of Satan" as
our Lord describes it. The Christian Church there would
be naturally exposed to the temptation to compromise, to be

---

8. the first and the last. Christ comforts the Christians of
Smyrna by reminding them that He, though Eternal, passed
through death; but His recovered life was proof that they too
would live again if only they were faithful.

9. I know. Not only I am aware of it but I know by
experience.

which say they are Jews. They pretend to be God's
chosen people, and out of zeal for God's truth persecuted the
Christians as Saul did; but they are shewn to be not a synagogue
of the Lord (Num. xvi. 3, 24) but one over which Satan presides
(John viii. 44).

10. the devil is about to cast. The Jews and heathen who
helped them were only instruments in the hands of the Devil, the
real author of religious persecution.

tribulation ten days. The limited time would help them to
bear it. It was not a long endless wearing persecution. See
2 Cor. iv. 17.

the crown of life. This is the positive of which "shall
not be hurt of the **second death**" is the negative. In the
eternal future there is something that answers to death here.
Its character no one knows but it is the loss of the crown of life,
i.e. possibly of the glorified body which means fulness of life.

true to Christ and yet not to draw down upon it the wrath of the world. This would be more especially the case if by "Satan's throne" is meant Caesar-worship. Easy-going tolerance, the right to go into the markets and buy whatever they pleased, whether it had been on a Pagan altar or not, the right to go into heathen society and mix freely with it—this was the danger of Pergamum.

And to the angel of the church in Pergamum write ;   12
These things saith he that hath the sharp two-edged sword : I know where thou dwellest, *even* where Satan's 13 throne is : and thou holdest fast my name, and didst not deny my faith, even in the days of Antipas my witness, my faithful one, who was killed among you, where Satan dwelleth. But I have a few things against thee, because 14 thou hast there some that hold the teaching of Balaam, who taught Balak to cast a stumblingblock before the children of Israel, to eat things sacrificed to idols, and to commit fornication. So hast thou also some that hold 15 the teaching of the Nicolaitans in like manner. Repent 16 therefore ; or else I come to thee quickly, and I will make war against them with the sword of my mouth. He that 17

---

12. he that hath the sharp two-edged sword. Our Lord reminds the Church that is tempted to take the easy line that His Word will cut their arguments to pieces and convict them.

13. even in the days of Antipas. Our Lord knows the difficulties of the situation and praises the courage that stood firm even when Antipas—the martyr and faithful one—suffered death. Of him nothing is known, save that he has the high honour of the Lord's own title (i. 5 and iii. 14).

14-15. the teaching of Balaam...the teaching of the Nicolaitans. There is no clear distinction between these. Balaam's sin was that of teaching "Balak how to beguile Israel into the double sin of idolatry and fornication," and that of Nicolas—possibly the proselyte of Antioch (Acts vi. 5)—was the same. There was therefore a party in the Church at Pergamum that made light of the necessary distinctions between Christians and heathen and looked upon the ordinances of the Council of Jerusalem (Acts xv. 29) as having no binding force. The Church had allowed this teaching to have wide influence, our Lord bids it repent and take swift action, otherwise He will be obliged to interfere.

hath an ear, let him hear what the Spirit saith to the
churches. To him that overcometh, to him will I give of
the hidden manna, and I will give him a white stone,
and upon the stone a new name written, which no one
knoweth but he that receiveth it.

18–29. *Letter to the Church in Thyatira.*

Thyatira was an inland city about 40 miles S.E. of Pergamum,
famous for its guilds, one of which was dyeing (Acts xvi. 14),
for its worship of the sun-god and for its Jewish or Persian
Sibyl who used to have her cult just outside the city. It is
possible that she may be the woman to whom our Lord
refers here. In that case like Simon Magus she must have
become a Christian, for the Jezebel here spoken of is a
member of the Church. The difficulty here was not due
to persecution but, as in Pergamum, to a strong worldly
wicked influence within the Church itself. Our Lord
declares that He will deal with this matter Himself. Some
terrible judgment will take place which will create wide-
spread alarm. To the faithful He promises great influence
and moral power.

18 And to the angel of the church in Thyatira write ;
These things saith the Son of God, who hath his eyes
like a flame of fire, and his feet are like unto burnished

---

17. the hidden manna...white stone. This is the description of the reward to be given to those who overcome these
seductions and immoral tendencies, those who will have the
courage to separate themselves from heathen society and ban-
quets; and it corresponds. " The hidden manna," referring
doubtless to the manna that was hidden away in the ark
(Exod. xvi. 23), is that peculiar and intimate fellowship with
Christ which comes in many ways, specially through the Eucharist.
The "white stone" has found a large variety of interpretations.
Only that will satisfy which explains its colour and the fact that
it was inscribed. Perhaps it refers to an engraved stone used
for magical purposes; and here, inscribed as it is with the new
name known only to the one who has it, represents that sense
of peculiar endearment to Christ, which a pet name always
indicates. Some however take the name as meaning the name
of God (iii. 12). In any case our Lord promises to those who
will separate from heathen society the blessing of His own society.
A white stone in its simplest idea means a pure imperishable
pledge of fellowship.

brass: I know thy works, and thy love and faith and 19
ministry and patience, and that thy last works are more
than the first. But I have *this* against thee, that thou 20
sufferest the woman Jezebel, which calleth herself a
prophetess; and she teacheth and seduceth my servants
to commit fornication, and to eat things sacrificed to
idols. And I gave her time that she should repent; and 21
she willeth not to repent of her fornication. Behold, I 22
do cast her into a bed, and them that commit adultery
with her into great tribulation, except they repent of her
works. And I will kill her children with death; and all 23
the churches shall know that I am he which searcheth
the reins and hearts: and I will give unto each one of
you according to your works. But to you I say, to the 24
rest that are in Thyatira, as many as have not this
teaching, which know not the deep things of Satan, as
they say; I cast upon you none other burden. Howbeit 25
that which ye have, hold fast till I come. And he that 26
overcometh, and he that keepeth my works unto the end,
to him will I give authority over the nations: and he 27

---

19. I know thy works etc. Our Lord's estimate of the
Church in Thyatira is a good one—love, faith, service, patience,
increasing abundance of good works; her only fault was lack of
moral courage in dealing with the bad woman who was ruining
so many of her members.

20. the woman Jezebel. It is noteworthy that this bad
influence was that of a woman who pretended to have great
spiritual power. Perhaps some member of the Church emulated
the Sibyl whose shrine was just outside the city walls or the
Sibyl herself may have been converted. By her cleverness she
shewed some knowledge of future events; her influence was
altogether worldly and immoral. Our Lord had tried to bring
her to repentance, but like Ahab's wife (1 Kings xvi. 31) she was
haughty and proud and exulted in her power over others.

22. I do cast her into a bed. The judgment that would
overtake her and her followers would be some terrible plague of
sickness, some pestilence so remarkable that all the other
churches would be struck by the evidence of the Lord's hand in
the matter.

26. to him will I give authority etc. The prize to those

shall rule them with a rod of iron, as the vessels of the
potter are broken to shivers ; as I also have received of
28
my Father : and I will give him the morning star. He
29
that hath an ear, let him hear what the Spirit saith to the
churches.

III. 1-6. *Letter to the Church in Sardis.*

Sardis, a flourishing manufacturing city, lay about 30 miles S.E.
of Thyatira. It had a bad name for luxury and loose
living. The city was probably too easy-going and careless
to trouble the Christians. The Church therefore was slack
and dead. It had a considerable reputation amongst the
neighbouring churches, but its influence in the city was nil.

3 And to the angel of the church in Sardis write ;

These things saith he that hath the seven Spirits of
God, and the seven stars : I know thy works, that thou
2 hast a name that thou livest, and thou art dead. Be
thou watchful, and stablish the things that remain, which
were ready to die : for I have found no works of thine
3 fulfilled before my God. Remember therefore how thou

---

who will keep separate and overcome the seductions to worldliness is in this case moral strength and influence. Even here
in this life there are abundant signs of it. History records again
and again the extraordinary power that has been wielded by
the pure. And in the future even more is promised (Lk. xix. 17).

28. the morning star. This influence is due to the possession
of Christ, Who is the Morning Star (xxii. 16), i.e. the secret of
the illumination and light that flashes forth from His servants.

III. 1. he that hath the seven Spirits. Christ describes
Himself here as One Who has intensity of Life and at the same
time a very near relation to His Church. He is able therefore to
quicken a dead Church.

I know thy works. Christ knows the reputation and knows
also how little right the Church has to it.

2. Be thou watchful. The Church was half asleep and
nothing was ever done perfectly. There were works, but everything was at loose ends and nothing could bear His examination.

3. Remember therefore how. Christ bids this sleepy
Church remember the enthusiasm with which she once received
the Gospel and wake up. If she fails, then there will be a sudden
judgment without warning.

hast received and didst hear ; and keep *it*, and repent.
If therefore thou shalt not watch, I will come as a thief,
and thou shalt not know what hour I will come upon
thee. But thou hast a few names in Sardis which did 4
not defile their garments : and they shall walk with me
in white ; for they are worthy. He that overcometh 5
shall thus be arrayed in white garments ; and I will in
no wise blot his name out of the book of life, and I will
confess his name before my Father, and before his
angels. He that hath an ear, let him hear what the 6
Spirit saith to the churches.

7-13. *Letter to the Church in Philadelphia.*

Philadelphia, some 30 miles from Sardis, was not a large city owing
to its frequent earthquakes. The worship of Dionysos (or
Bacchus) was its chief cult, but there was apparently no
persecution from the heathen though some opposition from
the Jews. The Christian Church was small and in the eyes
of the world feeble, but it was faithful and courageous and
so had the promise of unexpected influence and power even
over its adversaries the Jews. This promise, with a prediction
of some widespread judgment in which the Church would
be kept safe, was the object of the letter which contains no
warning and no threat.

And to the angel of the church in Philadelphia write ; 7
These things saith he that is holy, he that is true, he
that hath the key of David, he that openeth, and none

---

4. thou hast a few names. Not all Sardis was slack and
worldly.   There were a few, stern and pure in their lives, and
they should have the prize of glorified bodies.

5. arrayed in white garments.   This must mean the
resurrection glory in which the saints will be arrayed.   It is the
great reward and with it comes the confession on the part of
their High Priest that they have a right to it.   They had confessed Christ's name in Sardis and He, as He promised, would
confess their name before the Father (Matt. x. 32 and Luke xii. 8).

7. he that hath the key of David.   Christ describes Himself
as having the power to open or to shut, because He is going to
give this power to the Church in Philadelphia.

The reference here is to Isaiah xxii. 22 which gives a picture

8 shall shut, and that shutteth, and none openeth : I know thy works (behold, I have set before thee a door opened, which none can shut), that thou hast a little power, and didst keep my word, and didst not deny my name.

9 Behold, I give of the synagogue of Satan, of them which say they are Jews, and they are not, but do lie ; behold, I will make them to come and worship before thy feet, and

10 to know that I have loved thee. Because thou didst keep the word of my patience, I also will keep thee from the hour of trial, that *hour* which is to come upon the whole

11 world, to try them that dwell upon the earth. I come quickly : hold fast that which thou hast, that no one take

12 thy crown. He that overcometh, I will make him a pillar in the temple of my God, and he shall go out thence no more : and I will write upon him the name of my God, and the name of the city of my God, the new

---

of the prime minister Eliakim who had great influence and foreshadowed Christ to Whom power was given over all things in heaven and earth.

8. I know thy works. Though insignificant the Church was loyal and true, and in spite of provocation from the synagogue of Satan, i.e. the Jews, had borne brave witness to Christ.

9. I will make them to come. Through some means, the hard stiff diabolical opposition of the Jews was to come to an end and the Jews should seek the Christian Church for Baptism. Like a defeated enemy they would come begging for terms of peace. Dr Swete, quoting from the letter of St Ignatius written to this Church somewhat later, notes that the chief difficulty of the Church was through Judaizing Christians, as though there had been a large influx of converts some short time before.

11. I come quickly : hold fast that which thou hast. Christ came in some terrible judgment that befel this city and other parts of Asia Minor, and the Christians were warned to be faithful, remembering the promise that they would be kept.

12. I will make him a pillar. The reward here is that of strength to uplift others and also permanence. The whole fabric of the spiritual Temple of God is uplifted by innumerable pillars, fixed and eternal—the Saints of God—no sin or failure is henceforth possible.

I will write upon him the name of my God. Name stands for character and every conqueror bears a threefold

Jerusalem, which cometh down out of heaven from my
God, and mine own new name. He that hath an ear, let 13
him hear what the Spirit saith to the churches.

14-22.　*Letter to the Church in Laodicea.*

Laodicea was a wealthy manufacturing city of importance, but
like Philadelphia subject to earthquakes. Famous for its
woollen carpets and clothing. The Church, "perhaps founded
by Epaphras of Colossae," was known to St Paul, whose
circular letter, our Epistle to the Ephesians, was intended for Laodicea also. (Col. iv. 16.) When St John
wrote, the Church had fallen into a miserable condition of
blind self-conceit. There was no enthusiasm or energy but
a quiet self-complacency as though all were well. This
condition excites our Lord's wrath and contempt. It had
been better to have made no profession at all than to be so
self-satisfied with nothing. The letter advises the Laodiceans
to purchase love from Him Who alone can give it, good
works with which to cover their poor naked characters,
and above all grace to cure their blindness so that they
may see in what a woeful state they really are.

And to the angel of the church in Laodicea write ;　14
These things saith the Amen, the faithful and true
witness, the beginning of the creation of God : I know 15
thy works, that thou art neither cold nor hot : I would
thou wert cold or hot. So because thou art lukewarm, 16
and neither hot nor cold, I will spew thee out of my
mouth. Because thou sayest, I am rich, and have gotten 17
riches, and have need of nothing ; and knowest not that

character. (1) Love, this being the very Name of God.
(2) Fellowship, this being the name of the new Jerusalem, and
(3) Mystery, this being some fresh characteristic of Christ, His
new Name. See 1 John iii. 2 and Col. iii. 4

15. I would thou wert cold or hot. It is interesting to note
that the hot springs of Hierapolis, six miles off, when tapped at
Laodicea were lukewarm and therefore of no use for medicinal
purposes. The Laodicean would quite understand how hateful a
tepid spring is. And a tepid religion is to Christ a contemptible
thing. He Who was "the faithful," a Martyr steadfast unto death
(see *v.* 14), the One Whose zeal devoured Him, as the Apostles
noticed (John ii. 17), had no patience with a half-hearted religion.

thou art the wretched one and miserable and poor and
18 blind and naked : I counsel thee to buy of me gold
refined by fire, that thou mayest become rich ; and white
garments, that thou mayest clothe thyself, and *that* the
shame of thy nakedness be not made manifest; and
19 eyesalve to anoint thine eyes, that thou mayest see. As
many as I love, I reprove and chasten : be zealous
20 therefore, and repent. Behold, I stand at the door and
knock : if any man hear my voice and open the door, I
will come in to him, and will sup with him, and he with
21 me. He that overcometh, I will give to him to sit down
with me in my throne, as I also overcame, and sat down
22 with my Father in his throne. He that hath an ear, let
him hear what the Spirit saith to the churches.

PART II. CHRIST SEEN IN RELATION TO THE WORLD.

IV., V. i. *The Glory of God.*

IV. The scene now changes. From Earth we are transported to
Heaven. There in the very centre of the highest glory
of God we see the same Person, but this time imaged not
as the great King-Priest but as "a Lamb" that had passed
through Death. Christ is seen in His relation to the
world. No one has power to order history or the develop-
ment of God's purposes on earth but He Who is directing
the Church. Chapters iv. and v. must be taken in close
connection : the former shews us the Glory of God, the
latter the Glory of Christ in God.

18, 19. I counsel thee to buy of me. Three things were
needed (*a*) Moral wealth, i.e. Love ; (*b*) Spiritual clothing; Christ's
Righteousness imputed and imparted ; (*c*) Insight ; all these to be
obtained by prayer. And with them zeal, enthusiasm, devotion.
Note that in spite of Christ's contempt for their lukewarmness,
He still loved them.

21. I will give to him to sit down with me. This severe
letter is not without a promise to the conqueror and this is in
some ways the largest yet offered, a share in Christ's government
of the world, the high position coveted by St James and St John.

After these things I saw, and behold, a door opened in **4**
heaven, and the first voice which I heard, *a voice* as of a
trumpet speaking with me, one saying, Come up hither,
and I will shew thee the things which must come to pass
hereafter. Straightway I was in the Spirit: and behold, **2**
there was a throne set in heaven, and one sitting upon
the throne; and he that sat *was* to look upon like a **3**
jasper stone and a sardius: and *there was* a rainbow
round about the throne, like an emerald to look upon.
And round about the throne *were* four and twenty **4**
thrones: and upon the thrones *I saw* four and twenty
elders sitting, arrayed in white garments; and on their
heads crowns of gold. And out of the throne proceed **5**
lightnings and voices and thunders. And *there were*
seven lamps of fire burning before the throne, which are
the seven Spirits of God; and before the throne, as it **6**

IV. 1. I saw, and behold, a door. The Seer is enabled to
see this new vision partly through Divine help—a door was
opened—partly through an effort made on his own part in
response to the invitation "Come up hither." He is then shewn
the future, " the things which must come to pass hereafter."

2. there was a throne set. St John describes what he
saw, as best he can, by the help of the Spirit. There was a
Throne and on it a Person Whose appearance suggested spark-
ling crystal and deep red. This Person is not described, for "no
man hath seen God at any time," nor can see Him. The Throne
is set in a rainbow of emerald. These colours, white, red and
green, symbolize the purity, justice and mercy of God.

4. four and twenty elders. There are thrones about the
Great White Throne and on them representatives of humanity,
twelve representing the Jewish Church and twelve the Christian
Church. This appearance of men enthroned in the highest
glory must have impressed the Apostle deeply. They sit
undismayed by the peals of thunder and the frequent flashes of
lightning.

5. seven lamps of fire. Both the fire and water symbolize
the life of the Blessed Spirit Who illuminates and quickens.
See Acts ii. 3 and John vii. 38. In ch. xxii. 1 the glassy sea is
depicted as a river of water of life, bright as crystal, proceeding
out of the Throne of God.

were a glassy sea like unto crystal ; and in the midst of the
throne, and round about the throne, four living creatures
7 full of eyes before and behind.   And the first creature
was like a lion, and the second creature like a calf, and
the third creature had a face as of a man, and the fourth
8 creature *was* like a flying eagle.   And the four living
creatures, having each one of them six wings, are full of
eyes round about and within : and they have no rest day
and night, saying, Holy, holy, holy, *is* the Lord God, the
Almighty, which was and which is and which is to come.
9 And when the living creatures shaH give glory and
honour and thanks to him that sitteth on the throne, to
10 him that liveth for ever and ever, the four and twenty
elders shall fall down before him that sitteth on the
throne, and shall worship him that liveth for ever and
ever, and shall cast their crowns before the throne,
11 saying, Worthy art thou, our Lord and our God, to
receive the glory and the honour and the power : for
thou didst create all things, and because of thy will they
were, and were created.

---

6.   in the midst of the throne, and round about the throne.
The four living creatures express the glory of Nature, strength
as seen in the lion, endurance as seen in the calf, intelligence
as seen in man and quickness as seen in the eagle.   God is in
Nature and yet above it.

8.   they have no rest day and night.   These living creatures
are not dumb but have power to express themselves.   Their
great joy is in God's infinite perfections.

which is to come.   Every century brings with it a fuller
manifestation of the Being and Character of God, as is seen by
comparing the knowledge of the best now with what it was in
the Apostolic age.

11.   they were, and were created.   All things existed first in
the Mind of God, " *they were*," afterwards they " *were created*."

V. ii. *The Glory of Christ in God.*

This chapter must be taken in close connection with the preceding. The purpose of chapter iv. is to introduce fittingly the Mystery of the sealed book and of Him Who opens it. The Book represents the Plan of God for mankind. It is sealed because owing to sin it has never been made known. Again and again it has been arraigned as cruel, unjust and capricious because no one knew what it was. Now the Word of God has been expressed in human flesh. God has become Incarnate and the revelation of God's purposes is made clear. Christ and Christ alone can shew what God's mind is in history, for He and He alone is the Way.

And I saw in the right hand of him that sat on the 5 throne a book written within and on the back, close sealed with seven seals. And I saw a strong angel 2 proclaiming with a great voice, Who is worthy to open the book, and to loose the seals thereof? And no one in 3 the heaven, or on the earth, or under the earth, was able to open the book, or to look thereon. And I wept much, 4 because no one was found worthy to open the book, or to look thereon : and one of the elders saith unto me, Weep 5 not : behold, the Lion that is of the tribe of Judah, the Root of David, hath overcome, to open the book and the

---

V. 1. a book written within and on the back, i.e. a papyrus roll so full that the contents had overflowed to the other side of it. The book is not only full of God's purposes but more than full. There is not a jot that He has kept in reserve, and note that it lies *in* the right hand as though God were offering it to Humanity to read.

4. And I wept much. St John had often and often pondered over God's ways. Plagues, earthquakes, persecutions, the apparent inequalities of earth, the oppression of the powerful, the weakness of the good, what did it all mean? And all was written in the book of Destiny, but no one dare take it, and even had they been able to do so they could not have opened a single page.

5. the Lion...hath overcome. See Gen. xlix. 9 where Judah is spoken of as the Lion of the tribes. Our Lord as the Son of David realizes in Himself the distinctive quality of the tribe. In some way our Lord's sufferings and His conquest over them

6 seven seals thereof. And I saw in the midst of the
throne and of the four living creatures, and in the midst
of the elders, a Lamb standing, as though it had been
slain, having seven horns, and seven eyes, which are the
7 seven Spirits of God, sent forth into all the earth. And
he came, and he taketh *it* out of the right hand of him
8 that sat on the throne. And when he had taken the
book, the four living creatures and the four and twenty
elders fell down before the Lamb, having each one a
harp, and golden bowls full of incense, which are the
9 prayers of the saints. And they sing a new song, saying,
Worthy art thou to take the book, and to open the seals
thereof: for thou wast slain, and didst purchase unto
God with thy blood *men* of every tribe, and tongue, and
10 people, and nation, and madest them *to be* unto our God
a kingdom and priests; and they reign upon the earth.
11 And I saw, and I heard a voice of many angels round
about the throne and the living creatures and the elders;
and the number of them was ten thousand times ten

---

and Death enabled Him to gain, as the Head of Humanity,
such insight as not only to interpret the past but to carry
history onward through successive stages to the final goal.

6. in the midst of the throne. In the very centre of the
Highest Place in the Universe, Christ is seen imaged forth by a
sacrificed Lamb of infinite strength and infinite wisdom. He
has the Spirit, Who proceedeth from Him, and sees the inner-
most of all things. Van Eyck's great picture of The Adoration
of the Lamb, in the Church of St Bavon in Ghent, gives a wonderful representation of this.

8. which are the prayers of the saints. It is interesting to
note that according to this image, prayer goes up to God through
the Church, i.e. not singly but merged in the intercessions of the
great Universal Church. In this way it loses its selfishness and
is purged of all that makes it unacceptable.

9. they sing a new song. The joy of Creation at the book
of Destiny being read and its principles furthered by One so good
and loving as Christ expresses itself in bursts of song. The
song is new, for it is the song of redemption and of the establish-
ment of a new Kingdom of Humanity.

thousand, and thousands of thousands; saying with a 12
great voice, Worthy is the Lamb that hath been slain to
receive the power, and riches, and wisdom, and might,
and honour, and glory, and blessing.   And every created 13
thing which is in the heaven, and on the earth, and under
the earth, and on the sea, and all things that are in them,
heard I saying, Unto him that sitteth on the throne, and
unto the Lamb, *be* the blessing, and the honour, and the
glory, and the dominion, for ever and ever.   And the 14
four living creatures said, Amen.   And the elders fell
down and worshipped.

PART III. CHRIST DEVELOPS GOD'S PLAN.

VI. *The opening of the seals.*

The Book is God's plan for the world, the seals are the obstacles
which prevent it going forward, such as the obstinacy and
self-will of man.   The breaking of the seals is the over-
coming of these obstacles, and the Visions seen at the
breakings are the means which God uses.   The first seal
shews us the conquering Christ, the second War, the third
Famine, the fourth Death, the fifth Persecution, the sixth
Earthquake and the Last things.   We must remember that
war, famine, persecution and death were all terribly familiar
to St John, and he had been unable to harmonize them with
Christ's reign.   This Vision will help him.

And I saw when the Lamb opened one of the seven 6
seals, and I heard one of the four living creatures saying
as with a voice of thunder, Come.   And I saw, and 2

---

12.   **Worthy is the Lamb.**   The song of the angels differs
from that of men and nature.   In the latter the theme is the
redemption of the world, in the former the endowments of the
King.   The "taking the book" implied wisdom, power and
might.
13.   **And every created thing.**   Here angels and men unite
in one great chorus of thanksgiving and praise to the Eternal
Father and to the Lamb His Son.
VI. 1.   one of the four living creatures saying...Come.   The
living creatures express the very heart of Creation, its longing and
earnest expectation of redemption (Rom. viii. 22).   In spite

behold, a white horse, and he that sat thereon had a
bow ; and there was given unto him a crown : and he
came forth conquering, and to conquer.

3 And when he opened the second seal, I heard the
4 second living creature saying, Come. And another *horse*
came forth, a red horse : and to him that sat thereon it
was given to take peace from the earth, and that they
should slay one another : and there was given unto him
a great sword.

5 And when he opened the third seal, I heard the third
living creature saying, Come. And I saw, and behold, a
black horse ; and he that sat thereon had a balance in his
6 hand. And I heard as it were a voice in the midst of the
four living creatures saying, A measure of wheat for a
penny, and three measures of barley for a penny ; and
the oil and the wine hurt thou not.

7 And when he opened the fourth seal, I heard the voice
8 of the fourth living creature saying, Come. And I saw,

---

then of the horribleness of those events which are bound up with
the progress of the world, such as war, pestilence, etc., they cry
"Come." It would seem as though God Himself waited for
some response from Creation before allowing its scourges.

2. behold, a white horse. In spite of the high authority
which makes this vision represent the lust of conquest, it seems
better to take it as referring to the conquering Christ. The
first sight St John sees is that of his Lord. Victory belongs to
Him, though the path it takes is strange.

4. it was given to take peace. War is only by permission
of God Who hates it, though He hates the sin that causes it
infinitely more. "The Romish world and the Jewish world
were alike rent by civil war." "As early as the end of A.D. 68
a false Nero gained many adherents and caused wide-spread
alarm."

5. a black horse. Famine was one of the accompaniments of
war, and in these verses it is described as being so bad that a man's
daily wage only suffices to give him the poorest bread, he has
nothing to give wife or children unless he buys black bread
(barley). The cheapness of oil and wine, comparative luxuries,
only adds to the horror. A penny or *denarius* was an average
day's wage, and the measure or *chœnix* (marg.) very small.

and behold, a pale horse : and he that sat upon him, his
name was Death ; and Hades followed with him. And
there was given unto them authority over the fourth part
of the earth, to kill with sword, and with famine, and
with death, and by the wild beasts of the earth.

And when he opened the fifth seal, I saw underneath 9
the altar the souls of them that had been slain for the
word of God, and for the testimony which they held :
and they cried with a great voice, saying, How long, O 10
Master, the holy and true, dost thou not judge and
avenge our blood on them that dwell on the earth? And 11
there was given them to each one a white robe ; and it
was said unto them, that they should rest yet for a little
time, until their fellow-servants also and their brethren,
which should be killed even as they were, should be
fulfilled.

And I saw when he opened the sixth seal, and there 12
was a great earthquake ; and the sun became black as
sackcloth of hair, and the whole moon became as blood ;

---

8. a pale horse, i.e. a horse of ashen grey colour, the colour
of fright. Death rides this horse and behind Death follows the
world of Shades.

9. I saw underneath the altar. Note that earth gives no
invitation to the horror of persecution. There is no "Come."
Terrible as war, famine and death are, they have not the malice
nor diabolical hatred of persecution—and yet even persecution
paves the way for God's Kingdom. Here the cry for Christ's
advent comes from the souls of the martyrs who long for righteous
judgment on their oppressors. They are under the altar, because
that is where the blood of the victim—and the life lies in the
blood—would naturally be.

11. there was given them to each one a white robe.
We should like to know whether by this, which means that their
invisible souls had visible expression, is implied the resurrection
body. The usual opinion is that the new body is given on the
last great day. See iii. 4, 5 and vii. 9.

12. I saw when he opened the sixth seal. The last obstacle
is overcome and all the terrors of the last judgment are revealed.
Cp. this vision with our Lord's predictions of the end of all
things, espec. Mark xiii. 24–37.

13 and the stars of the heaven fell unto the earth, as a fig tree casteth her unripe figs, when she is shaken of a great
14 wind. And the heaven was removed as a scroll when it is rolled up ; and every mountain and island were moved
15 out of their places. And the kings of the earth, and the princes, and the chief captains, and the rich, and the strong, and every bondman and freeman, hid themselves
16 in the caves and in the rocks of the mountains ; and they say to the mountains and to the rocks, Fall on us, and hide us from the face of him that sitteth on the throne,
17 and from the wrath of the Lamb : for the great day of their wrath is come ; and who is able to stand?

PART IV. INTERLUDE. CHRIST PROTECTS HIS OWN FROM THE JUDGMENTS THAT FALL ON THE WORLD.

VII. A question naturally arises here which this chapter answers. What would be the position of the Christians in these terrible scourges of war, pestilence and famine? Would they fall under the threatened judgments? For reply we see a picture of judgment held back till the security of the saints shall have been guaranteed. This is effected by the sealing of God's people. This sealing does not mean that they are protected from, but protected in, the judgments that follow. They are in the great tribulation but come out of it without harm, nay, they are purified through it. So this chapter comes as an episode before the breaking of the seventh seal.

7 After this I saw four angels standing at the four corners of the earth, holding the four winds of the earth,

---

16. Fall on us, and hide us. The sinful are always as much appalled by the face of triumphant Purity as the Saints are rejoiced by it. To the one it necessarily means the overthrow and ruin of all they care for, to the other it means the vindication of all they have longed for. Note the expression—"the wrath of the Lamb." Perhaps nothing is more heart-searching than righteous anger in the gentlest. None can stand unconvicted before it. See Hos. x. 8 ; Gen. iii. 8 and Luke xxiii. 30.

17. See Joel ii. 11 and Zeph. i. 14.

VII. 1. the four winds. These represent the judgments of which chapter vi. has spoken. There is a pause before they are allowed to begin, and during this time the Saints are sealed.

that no wind should blow on the earth, or on the sea, or
upon any tree. And I saw another angel ascend from 2
the sunrising, having the seal of the living God: and he
cried with a great voice to the four angels, to whom it
was given to hurt the earth and the sea, saying, Hurt not 3
the earth, neither the sea, nor the trees, till we shall have
sealed the servants of our God on their foreheads. And 4
I heard the number of them which were sealed, a hundred
and forty and four thousand, sealed out of every tribe of
the children of Israel.

Of the tribe of Judah *were* sealed twelve thousand :   5
Of the tribe of Reuben twelve thousand :
Of the tribe of Gad twelve thousand :
Of the tribe of Asher twelve thousand :   6
Of the tribe of Naphtali twelve thousand :
Of the tribe of Manasseh twelve thousand :
Of the tribe of Simeon twelve thousand :   7
Of the tribe of Levi twelve thousand :
Of the tribe of Issachar twelve thousand :
Of the tribe of Zebulun twelve thousand :   8
Of the tribe of Joseph twelve thousand :
Of the tribe of Benjamin *were* sealed twelve thousand.

---

3. Hurt not the earth...till we shall have sealed. See
Ezek. ix. 4 where the righteous are marked with a mark—which
strangely enough was cruciform—to prevent their being massacred.
Here they are marked with a signet ring. The symbolism is plain.
God's care is secured to them, so that like the three saints in
the furnace of fire they receive no hurt. Dan. iii. 27.

4. I heard the number. The sum is a multiple of twelve
and seems to express the fact that the true Israel of God is
multiplied a thousandfold.

5. Of the tribe of Judah. Note that Judah stands first here,
though fourth in order of birth; and Levi eighth, whilst Dan is
omitted altogether and Ephraim is swallowed up in Joseph.
These alterations are extremely interesting, suggesting that in the
mind of the Seer the priestly tribe had fallen morally below
many of their brethren, and by their opposition to Christ had lost
their preeminent place. Judah is naturally first, as Christ "sprang

9 After these things I saw, and behold, a great multitude,
which no man could number, out of every nation, and of
all tribes and peoples and tongues, standing before the
throne and before the Lamb, arrayed in white robes, and
10 palms in their hands ; and they cry with a great voice,
saying, Salvation unto our God which sitteth on the
11 throne, and unto the Lamb. And all the angels were
standing round about the throne, and *about* the elders
and the four living creatures ; and they fell before the
throne on their faces, and worshipped God, saying,
12 Amen : Blessing, and glory, and wisdom, and thanksgiving, and honour, and power, and might, *be* unto our
13 God for ever and ever. Amen. And one of the elders
answered, saying unto me, These which are arrayed in
the white robes, who are they, and whence came they?
14 And I say unto him, My lord, thou knowest. And he
said to me, These are they which come out of the great
tribulation, and they washed their robes, and made them
15 white in the blood of the Lamb. Therefore are they
before the throne of God ; and they serve him day and

---

out of Judah." Why Dan is omitted is not clear; the Rabbinic
association of the tribe with idolatry and apostasy does not seem
to be a sufficient reason.

9. and behold, a great multitude. This is the second part of
the one vision expressing the same thought only from a different
point of view. In the first we see God's own people secure in
the great tribulation, in the second they have come out of it.
There they are clearly defined and marked out from the world
as the true Israel ; here they are a great numberless multitude
composed of every nationality. There nothing is said about
palms and white robes because they are in the midst of the conflict ; here they have gained their reward. So the episode
teaches two lessons, one of preservation and the other of complete
redemption.

14. made them white. The blood of Christ represents the
spirit of Christ's self-sacrifice. By the surrender of their lives the
Saints have been rid of every vestige of selfishness and therefore
are white even before the Throne of God.

night in his temple : and he that sitteth on the throne
shall spread his tabernacle over them.   They shall hunger 16
no more, neither thirst any more ; neither shall the sun
strike upon them, nor any heat . for the Lamb which is 17
in the midst of the throne shall be their shepherd, and
shall guide them unto fountains of waters of life : and
God shall wipe away every tear from their eyes.

PART V.   CHRIST SUMMONS THE WORLD TO SURRENDER.

VIII., IX.   *The sounding of the trumpets.*

VIII.   The relation between the seals and the trumpets is very
close.   The breaking of the sixth seal ushered in the final
judgment of the world, the breaking of the seventh is followed
by silence expressing the Sabbath stillness which comes after
the awful storm of judgment.   The sealed book is now done
with.   The destiny of mankind has been unfolded.   But
St John has only learnt one aspect of the Divine judgments,
namely as instruments by which the obstacles of man's sin
are overcome.   He is to learn the same lesson under another
image, that of the trumpet.   The trumpet note is a challenge
to the world to surrender, as it was at Jericho.   They are
the notes sounded by the advancing host of Christ's unseen
army.   Plagues, wars, persecutions are not only Divine
instruments by which the world is gradually being brought
right, but appeals to its conscience.

And when he opened the seventh seal, there followed a 8
silence in heaven about the space of half an hour.   And I 2
saw the seven angels which stand before God ; and there
were given unto them seven trumpets.

And another angel came and stood over the altar, 3

---

15.   **he that sitteth...shall spread his tabernacle.**   The
Saints are now eternally protected from all evil by the over-
shadowing Presence of the Most High.

17.   **for the Lamb...shall be their shepherd.**   Strength,
refreshment and joy are the notes of the new life.   As they
enter into the near Presence of God they are taught the mysteries
which underlie sorrow and pain, and are freed from all sorrow.

VIII. 1.   **there followed a silence in heaven.**   A time during
which the Seer could take in all that he had heard and seen.
"A temporary suspension of revelation" for thought.

having a golden censer; and there was given unto him much incense, that he should add it unto the prayers of all the saints upon the golden altar which was before the

4 throne. And the smoke of the incense, with the prayers of the saints, went up before God out of the angel's hand.

5 And the angel taketh the censer; and he filled it with the fire of the altar, and cast it upon the earth: and there followed thunders, and voices, and lightnings, and an earthquake.

6 And the seven angels which had the seven trumpets prepared themselves to sound.

7 And the first sounded, and there followed hail and fire, mingled with blood, and they were cast upon the earth: and the third part of the earth was burnt up, and the third part of the trees was burnt up, and all green grass was burnt up.

3–5. there was given unto him much incense. This explains the mysterious relation between prayer and judgment. The angel who stands like a priest to offer incense has in his bowl not only incense but the prayers of the Saints. The incense doubtless represents the merits of Christ which alone make our prayers of any value. (See Eph. v. 2 and 1 John ii. 1 foll.; Rom. viii. 34 and Heb. xii. 25.) After offering these before God, he filled the empty bowl with coals from the fire of the altar and flung them down upon the earth, with terrible consequences. This seems to be the Divine response to prayer. We pray that the world may become better, not realizing that its betterment can only come through disasters. This too was a revelation to St John.

7. And the first sounded, and there followed hail. This reminds us of the seventh plague, but refers no doubt to some actual devastation which the Apostle had in mind. Here the heavens, instead of giving refreshing showers, send down hail and fire mingled with blood which is accompanied by terrible drought. "Blood-red rain is not unknown in nature; in the spring of 1901 the daily journals contained accounts of this phenomenon in Italy...the air being full of particles of fine red sand from Sahara." Such a sanding of the earth would have a blasting effect on the vegetation. Renan notes that there were awful storms during A.D. 63, 68 and 69.

And the second angel sounded, and as it were a great **8** mountain burning with fire was cast into the sea : and the third part of the sea became blood ; and there died **9** the third part of the creatures which were in the sea, *even* they that had life ; and the third part of the ships was destroyed.

And the third angel sounded, and there fell from **10** heaven a great star, burning as a torch, and it fell upon the third part of the rivers, and upon the fountains of the waters ; and the name of the star is called Wormwood : **11** and the third part of the waters became wormwood ; and many men died of the waters, because they were made bitter.

And the fourth angel sounded, and the third part of **12** the sun was smitten, and the third part of the moon, and the third part of the stars; that the third part of them should be darkened, and the day should not shine for the third part of it, and the night in like manner.

And I saw, and I heard an eagle, flying in mid heaven, **13**

---

8. a great mountain burning with fire was cast into the sea. In the year A.D. 79 the Great Eruption of Vesuvius took place, accounts of which would reach St John. What did it mean ? Here is the explanation. It was a Voice of God summoning the world to repentance, just as the fall of the Tower of Siloam was. See our Lord's teaching, Luke xiii. 4.

10. there fell from heaven a great star. This judgment is the poisoning of the founts and rivers. The plagues and pestilences, the fevers and agues that lurked in marshes and foul springs were not accidental, but allowed by God to awe mankind and to urge them to consider their ways. " In Rome a pestilence had carried off tens of thousands of the citizens." What was the cause? Was Christ reigning ? Yes, this is His trumpet appeal.

12. the third part of the sun was smitten. In those days eclipses of sun and moon were regarded with terror as betokening terrible judgments to come. Men were perpetually talking about them. St John explains that they are meant to make men think, to lead them to repentance.

13. I heard an eagle. This was an angel pictured as an eagle who declares to men that the physical convulsions and

saying with a great voice, Woe, woe, woe, for them that
dwell on the earth, by reason of the other voices of the
trumpet of the three angels, who are yet to sound.

> **IX. 1–11.** The judgment described in these verses is not physical
> but spiritual; for the star is an angel having the key of the
> pit of the abyss, and though the judgment is described under
> the image of a plague of locusts, yet it is made plain that
> the writer is referring to an army of evil spirits under their
> great Captain, the Destroyer. One marked feature of the
> times in which St John lived was its sadness, gloom, de-
> pression. Suicide was frequent, but the distress that led men
> to think of killing themselves combined with the cowardice
> that held them back was still more common. He could not
> help noticing this and contrasting it with the joy of the
> Christians. In this section he gives the explanation that
> God gave him as to how it arose.

9   And the fifth angel sounded, and I saw a star from
heaven fallen unto the earth: and there was given to him
2 the key of the pit of the abyss. And he opened the pit of
the abyss; and there went up a smoke out of the pit, as
the smoke of a great furnace; and the sun and the air
3 were darkened by reason of the smoke of the pit. And
out of the smoke came forth locusts upon the earth; and
power was given them, as the scorpions of the earth have
4 power. And it was said unto them that they should not
hurt the grass of the earth, neither any green thing,
neither any tree, but only such men as have not the seal

---

prodigies are as nothing compared with the spiritual judgments
that are to take place.

IX. 1. I saw a star from heaven. See Is. xiv. 12 and Lk. x.
18 where the star is personified as Satan. Note he has no power
in himself to summon his evil followers, this is given to him by
One who has the keys of the abyss. Matt. xvi. 19; Rev. i. 15.

3. And out of the smoke came forth locusts. The evil
spirits are described as locusts and scorpions, the former having
power to rob vegetation of life, the latter having power to inflict
torture. Spiritual Death and Pain are the results of the working
of the evil spirits.

4, 5. only such men as have not the seal. These dark
gloomy demons have no power over the Christians, only over

of God on their foreheads. And it was given them that 5
they should not kill them, but that they should be
tormented five months : and their torment was as the
torment of a scorpion, when it striketh a man. And in 6
those days men shall seek death, and shall in no wise
find it ; and they shall desire to die, and death fleeth
from them. And the shapes of the locusts were like unto 7
horses prepared for war ; and upon their heads as it were
crowns like unto gold, and their faces were as men's faces.
And they had hair as the hair of women, and their teeth 8
were as *the teeth* of lions. And they had breastplates, as 9
it were breastplates of iron ; and the sound of their wings
was as the sound of chariots, of many horses rushing to
war. And they have tails like unto scorpions, and stings ; 10
and in their tails is their power to hurt men five months.
They have over them as king the angel of the abyss : his 11

---

those living in the world. Our Lord gave His disciples "authority
to tread upon serpents and scorpions and over all the power of
the enemy" (Lk. x. 19). The torment extends over five months,
the time being indefinite (see Matt. xxv. 15 ; Lk. xii. 6) and
therefore adding to the horror.

6. they shall desire to die. Nothing more horrible than
the wish to die when united to the fear that prevents a man
from taking steps towards it.

7-10. the shapes of the locusts. In this passage St John
tries to describe the malice and wickedness of the evil spirits.
They are determined and expect to conquer, and so were crowned.
They had a bad man's resolution combined with a bad woman's
fascinating sensuality. Once they had hold of their victims they
never let them go, for they had teeth like lions. They were as
implacable as though they were clad in steel, and as noisy and
threatening as though there were millions of them. They never
attacked in a straightforward way but always indirectly. Cp.
Joel ii. 7.

11. They have over them as king. There is a kind of
authority even in Hell. These spirits cannot venture forth
except at the bidding of their leader, and he has no power
unless given him by God. His name, Destroyer or Destruction,
describes the work in which he is engaged, which is to destroy all
good.

name in Hebrew is Abaddon, and in the Greek *tongue* he
hath the name Apollyon.

12 The first Woe is past : behold, there come yet two
Woes hereafter.

> **IX. 13–21.** Wars, plagues, famines, gloom and depression,
> were all prevalent signs of the times in which St John lived.
> There was one other, terror of some terrible incursion of
> barbarians, like the Parthians. This was to come, as history
> tells us. The Vision that follows the blast of the sixth
> trumpet shews it to the Seer. So far this scourge has been
> kept back by the power of God, but now God removes the
> restraint and a countless host of cavalry appears which does
> enormous destruction amongst mankind. Again and again
> in history, as in the Turkish invasions or the French Revo-
> lution, some abnormal judgment invades like a flood some
> part of the world. At such times it seems as though Satan
> were master, but the Seer shews us that this is only permitted
> of God and is really his trumpet blast summoning the world
> to surrender. It is interesting to find in the Sibylline
> Oracles the following : " towards evening war will arise and
> the great fugitive of Rome will raise the sword and *with
> many myriads of men ride through the Euphrates.*"

13 And the sixth angel sounded, and I heard a voice from
14 the horns of the golden altar which is before God, one
saying to the sixth angel, which had the trumpet, Loose
the four angels which are bound at the great river
15 Euphrates. And the four angels were loosed, which had
been prepared for the hour and day and month and year,

---

12. The first Woe. What he has just described is far worse
than any physical judgment and so is here named as " The first
Woe." There are two others like it which are to follow.

13. I heard a voice. This voice proceeds from the altar of
incense and is therefore a prayer of the Church calling for
judgment on the wickedness of the world. Anything is better
than the triumph of ungodliness.

14. Loose the four angels. These angels of destruction are
represented as being on the confines of the Empire. Euphrates
represented the extreme limit of Israel's dominions. The peril
comes from without the Roman Empire, perhaps from the dreaded
Parthians.

15. which had been prepared for the hour and day.
Nothing happens by chance. Even these terrible disorders are

that they should kill the third part of men. And the 16
number of the armies of the horsemen was twice ten
thousand times ten thousand: I heard the number of
them. And thus I saw the horses in the vision, and 17
them that sat on them, having breastplates *as* of fire
and of hyacinth and of brimstone : and the heads of the
horses are as the heads of lions ; and out of their mouths
proceedeth fire and smoke and brimstone. By these 18
three plagues was the third part of men killed, by the fire
and the smoke and the brimstone, which proceeded out
of their mouths. For the power of the horses is in their 19
mouth, and in their tails : for their tails are like unto
serpents, and have heads ; and with them they do hurt.
And the rest of mankind, which were not killed with 20
these plagues, repented not of the works of their hands,
that they should not worship devils, and the idols of gold,
and of silver, and of brass, and of stone, and of wood ;
which can neither see, nor hear, nor walk : and they 21
repented not of their murders, nor of their sorceries, nor
of their fornication, nor of their thefts.

---

timed to meet certain outbreaks of spiritual wickedness, though
no one but God knows the moment (Mk. xiii. 32).

16. the number of the armies. Two hundred million
represented the countless hosts of barbarians that burst in upon
the civilized world.

17. I saw the horses in the vision. The horses had the
heads of lions and long dragon-like tails by which they inflicted
the worst damage. The breastplates of the riders seemed to be
made of fire, hyacinth and brimstone, i.e. they suggested the
evil of the bottomless pit from which they proceeded as well as
the means by which the devastation was effected.

20. the rest of mankind...repented not. The design of
these terrible scourges which now and again afflict mankind is to
produce repentance, to make men ashamed of their idolatry and
their sins, but it fails.

PART VI. INTERLUDE. CHRIST ASSURES THE CHURCH THAT
THE END OF THESE JUDGMENTS IS NEAR AND THAT HE
WILL PROTECT HIS OWN.

X., XI. (1-14).   *Second Episode.*

X. Between the 6th and 7th trumpets as between the 6th and 7th
seals there is an Episode which in this case consists of two
Visions, the one that of the little Book in this chapter, the
other that of the two witnesses in chapter xi. Both are
very difficult to interpret. In this chapter the main
thought is that of the nearness of the end. The Mighty
Angel declares that "time shall be no longer." The mystery
of God is finished. It might be supposed that the Revelation
would end, but to the Seer is given another book of prophecy
which concerns many peoples, nations and kings.

10   And I saw another strong angel coming down out of
heaven, arrayed with a cloud ; and the rainbow was upon
his head, and his face was as the sun, and his feet as
2 pillars of fire ; and he had in his hand a little book open.
and he set his right foot upon the sea, and his left upon
3 the earth; and he cried with a great voice, as a lion
roareth   and when he cried, the seven thunders uttered
4 their voices. And when the seven thunders uttered *their
voices*, I was about to write : and I heard a voice from
heaven saying, Seal up the things which the seven
5 thunders uttered, and write them not. And the angel

X. 1. another strong angel. From the fact that the rainbow
was upon his head and his face shone as the sun, it might be
supposed that this Angel was Christ, but his action and still
more the word " another " make it quite clear that this is not so.
There are dignities amongst the angelic body and this Angel is
one of the highest order.

2. a little book. A small papyrus roll. For the figure cp.
Ezek. iii. 1-5 ; 2 Esdras xiv. 38, 39 and Collect for 2nd Sunday
in Advent.

4. the seven thunders. See Jn. xii. 29. The language
like thunder in sound was intelligible to the prophet but he was
not allowed to reveal what he heard. Like St Paul (2 Cor.
xii. 4) they were "unspeakable words which it is not lawful for a
man to utter."

which I saw standing upon the sea and upon the earth
lifted up his right hand to heaven, and sware by him that **6**
liveth for ever and ever, who created the heaven and the
things that are therein, and the earth and the things that
are therein, and the sea and the things that are therein,
that there shall be time no longer: but in the days of the **7**
voice of the seventh angel, when he is about to sound,
then is finished the mystery of God, according to the
good tidings which he declared to his servants the
prophets. And the voice which I heard from heaven, *I* **8**
heard it again speaking with me, and saying, Go, take
the book which is open in the hand of the angel that
standeth upon the sea and upon the earth. And I went **9**
unto the angel, saying unto him that he should give me
the little book. And he saith unto me, Take it, and eat
it up; and it shall make thy belly bitter, but in thy mouth
it shall be sweet as honey. And I took the little book **10**
out of the angel's hand, and ate it up; and it was in my
mouth sweet as honey: and when I had eaten it, my
belly was made bitter. And they say unto me, Thou **11**
must prophesy again over many peoples and nations and
tongues and kings.

---

6. time no longer. Perhaps the margin "delay" better
expresses the thought. See 2 Pet. iii. 3 ff. for the feeling
common amongst Christians. This assured them that the end
would at last come and God's wonderful purpose in the
evolution of human history would be unfolded.

8. Go, take the book. Though not allowed to reveal the
mysterious thunders, he has a message to give which is contained
in the little book the angel had.

10. it was in my mouth sweet. The first impression of the
book was delightful because it spoke of the end, but when
St John thought of all that must first come, the conflict and the
pain, he realized how bitter its thought was. And yet he was
obliged to proclaim its message.

XI. 1–14. There is no doubt a likeness here as in the last chapter
to the two Episodes of chapter vii. The preservation of the
saints in the midst of terrible persecution is what is intended.
The Temple of God, the Christian Church, is measured,
that is, it is protected, but the court without the Temple of
the holy city is given over to the heathen. Perhaps this
refers to a difference in treatment of the Christians as
distinct from the Jews. The true Israel is preserved, the
old Israel is trodden under foot. The persecution only
lasts for a time, and during that time the Church witnesses
for her Lord. And her witness is sustained by miracles, but
the time comes when God's purpose is fulfilled and the
witness is silenced. Christianity seems to be dead but is not
really so, for a new life is given and the confession of Christ
is more remarkable than ever. The whole earth seems to
be shaken by it, judgment follows and even the unbelievers
give glory to Him.

11 And there was given me a reed like unto a rod : and
one said, Rise, and measure the temple of God, and the
2 altar, and them that worship therein. And the court
which is without the temple leave without, and measure it
not ; for it hath been given unto the nations : and the holy
city shall they tread under foot forty and two months.
3 And I will give unto my two witnesses, and they shall

XI. 1. **there was given me a reed.** St John is here no longer
a witness but an actor. He is to measure the temple, the altar
and worshippers. Cp. Zech. ii. 1. This measurement is not
with a view to obtain their size but rather to draw a protecting
line about them. It is impossible not to see here a reference
to the destruction of Jerusalem in A.D. 70. But that is simply
the image of something wider and even more terrible in its
far-reaching effects. The Temple-altar worshippers represent
the inner shrine of Religion, i.e. the pure Christian faith.

2. the court which is without. This represents the outer
body from which Christianity sprang, i.e. Judaism which had
become formal and hard. Being profaned and trodden under
foot it would be despised by the nations but not for ever. The
42 months which was the period of the domination of Antiochus
Epiphanes (referred to rather differently in Dan. vii. 25 and xii. 7)
represents an incomplete time. As St Paul writes (Rom. xi.
12, 15, 26) a day will come when "all Israel shall be saved."

3. my two witnesses. This is admittedly difficult. There may

prophesy a thousand two hundred and threescore days, clothed in sackcloth. These are the two olive trees and 4 the two candlesticks, standing before the Lord of the earth. And if any man desireth to hurt them, fire 5 proceedeth out of their mouth, and devoureth their enemies : and if any man shall desire to hurt them, in this manner must he be killed. These have the power to 6 shut the heaven, that it rain not during the days of their prophecy : and they have power over the waters to turn them into blood, and to smite the earth with every plague, as often as they shall desire. And when they shall have 7 finished their testimony, the beast that cometh up out of the abyss shall make war with them, and overcome them, and kill them. And their dead bodies *lie* in the street of 8 the great city, which spiritually is called Sodom and Egypt,

---

be a reference to Moses and Elijah ; or to the Baptist and Christ, the faithful witness; or to St Paul and St Peter; or to the witness of the Apostles and disciples who went out two by two (Luke x. 1), or perhaps to all these as symbolising the witness of the Church. Or there may be a reference to the testimony of truth which is invalid unless it is supported by two witnesses. The main thought is that during a time of general persecution there will be a confession of Christ made by the Church, shewing every evidence of repentance, for 1260 days, i.e. roughly speaking the 3½ years of heathen domination.

4. These are the two olive trees. Cp. Zech. iv. 1–3 and 11–14. The one image shews that the witnesses have their inspiration of God, the other that they are the light of the world.

5. fire proceedeth out of their mouth. An allusion to 2 Kings ·i. 10. For the spiritual application see Heb. iv. 12 ; Acts xxiv. 25 and Luke xxi. 15.

6. These have the power. The Church through prayer may exercise wide and strange powers. See Matt. xxi. 21 and Jas. v. 17.

7. when they shall have finished their testimony. As long as their witness is needed they are under God's protection and cannot be touched ; but as soon as the testimony of the Church for that particular age has been adequately given, then Satan is allowed to silence the Christian faith.

8. their dead bodies lie in the street of the great city... called Sodom and Egypt. Every indignity is offered to the slain

9 where also their Lord was crucified. And from among
the peoples and tribes and tongues and nations do *men*
look upon their dead bodies three days and a half, and
10 suffer not their dead bodies to be laid in a tomb. And
they that dwell on the earth rejoice over them, and make
merry ; and they shall send gifts one to another ; because
these two prophets tormented them that dwell on the
11 earth. And after the three days and a half the breath of
life from God entered into them, and they stood upon
their feet ; and great fear fell upon them which beheld
12 them. And they heard a great voice from heaven saying
unto them, Come up hither. And they went up into
heaven in the cloud ; and their enemies beheld them.
13 And in that hour there was a great earthquake, and the
tenth part of the city fell ; and there were killed in the
earthquake seven thousand persons : and the rest were
affrighted, and gave glory to the God of heaven.
14   The second Woe is past . behold, the third Woe
cometh quickly.

Church. The city in the mind of St John is Jerusalem ; but
it also represents the world that is opposed to Christ. This
world is as wicked as Sodom, as oppressive as Egypt, as hard
and cruel as Jerusalem where the Lord was crucified.

10. they that dwell on the earth rejoice. The world now
triumphs over the death of Christianity. For a short time—three
and a half years represents an incomplete period—there is great
rejoicing, because the rebuke of sin is no longer heard.

11–13. And after the three days and a half. The persecuted
Church now rises stronger than ever, with increased power and
energy. Our Lord's Resurrection and Ascension is spiritually
repeated. As then there was an earthquake, so now there is a
quaking of people's hearts. Paganism receives a severe check,
part of its life is altogether overthrown and a deep religious fear
is everywhere awakened.

PART VII. THE SEVENTH TRUMPET OR THIRD WOE.

XI. 15-19.   *The final triumph.*

The contrast between the effect of the seventh seal and that of
the seventh trumpet is most marked.   The seventh seal was
followed by silence, the seventh trumpet by the glorious
sound of adoration and worship.   The Seer hears what the
issue of these terrible appeals to the conscience of the world
is.   Just as at the seventh circuit of the city of Jericho the
walls fell down flat, so now the seventh appeal to surrender
is followed by a chorus of praise announcing that the world
has rendered.

And the seventh angel sounded; and there followed 15
great voices in heaven, and they said, The kingdom of
the world is become *the kingdom* of our Lord, and of his
Christ: and he shall reign for ever and ever. And the 16
four and twenty elders, which sit before God on their
thrones, fell upon their faces, and worshipped God,
saying, We give thee thanks, O Lord God, the Almighty, 17
which art and which wast; because thou hast taken thy
great power, and didst reign. And the nations were 18
wroth, and thy wrath came, and the time of the dead to
be judged, and *the time* to give their reward to thy
servants the prophets, and to the saints, and to them
that fear thy name, the small and the great; and to
destroy them that destroy the earth.

And there was opened the temple of God that is in 19
heaven ; and there was seen in his temple the ark of his
covenant ; and there followed lightnings, and voices, and
ᵗhunders, and an earthquake, and great hail.

---

15. **The kingdom of the world is become the kingdom of
our Lord, and of his Christ**. The end of wars, pestilences,
persecutions is now seen in the reign of the Father (our Lord)
and His Christ, i.e. His Anointed Son. See Ps. ii. and
Acts iv. 26.

18. **And the nations were wroth, and thy wrath came**.
This is the explanation of the great judgments of God; it was
the Divine response to the rebellion of man.

19. **and there was seen in his temple the ark of his
covenant**. In the old Temple the ark was never seen except by

BOOK II. CHAPTERS XII.—XXII.

The object of this second volume is to shew the part which
Pagan Rome plays in the onward progress of Christianity.
Satan uses both the political and religious powers of the
Empire in his useless endeavour to conquer the Christian
Faith. Though he is allowed to do much harm, in the end
he is destroyed, and the Church, purified and strengthened,
is seen in all her glory and triumph.

PART I. REVELATION OF THE MYSTERY OF WICKEDNESS
THAT LIES HIDDEN BEHIND THE OPPOSITION OF THE
WORLD.

XII. This new division of the Book shews us what lies behind the
heavy judgments of God which the first part has described.
Behind the hostility of the world there is the Dragon; and this
Vision shews us the conflict between the Dragon and the
Church. We now see that the war is not one merely
between evil and good, but between the Evil Spirit and the
Spirit of God in the Church.

12 And a great sign was seen in heaven; a woman arrayed
with the sun, and the moon under her feet, and upon her
2 head a crown of twelve stars; and she was with child:

---

the High Priest once in the year. From the second Temple it
was absent, having probably perished when Nebuchadnezzar
burnt the Temple (2 Kings xxv. 9). In the new Temple of God
it is seen again, not in figure but reality. Christ is the ark
of the covenant of God and the last judgment is accompanied by
some fresh revelation of His Glory amidst "the solemn salvos
so to speak of the artillery of Heaven." The first part of the
book ends here. Had nothing followed the Visions given would
have been a complete prophecy. A new division begins with
chapter xii.

XII. 1. a great sign was seen. The word "sign," so often
used by St John in his Gospel, means a symbol; and the symbol
here seen is a woman, representing the Jewish Church. She is
arrayed with the sun, i.e. robed in light, and has the moon under
her feet, i.e. she is unchangeable in the Truth she holds. Her
crown consists of the very best of men, the saints of the Old
Testament.

2. she was with child. The Jewish Church is often described
as a travailing woman (see Micah iv. 10; Is. xxvi. 17). See too

and she crieth out, travailing in birth, and in pain to be
delivered. And there was seen another sign in heaven ; 3
and behold, a great red dragon, having seven heads and
ten horns, and upon his heads seven diadems. And his 4
tail draweth the third part of the stars of heaven, and did
cast them to the earth : and the dragon stood before the
woman which was about to be delivered, that when she
was delivered, he might devour her child. And she was 5
delivered of a son, a man child, who is to rule all the
nations with a rod of iron : and her child was caught up
unto God, and unto his throne. And the woman fled into 6
the wilderness, where she hath a place prepared of God,
that there they may nourish her a thousand two hundred
and threescore days.

And there was war in heaven : Michael and his angels 7
going forth to war with the dragon ; and the dragon

John xvi. 21 where our Lord uses the same thought.   Here
it pictures the Jewish Church after the Incarnation bearing in her
womb the Christian Church and awaiting Christ's Birth.

3. another sign in heaven. Here follows a picture of the
great antagonist—a great dragon (Gen. iii. 1 and v. 9), red
because he is a murderer from the beginning (John viii. 44) with
seven heads denoting intellectual power and seven diadems
shewing his victorious might.   His work is done in a cunning
underhand way "by his tail," by which he is able to influence a
host of angels who were ready to follow him.

5. she was delivered of a son, a man child. This refers to
the birth of the Christ, Who after a short ministry ascended on
high to His throne.

6. the woman fled into the wilderness. The flight of
Christ into Egypt, his sojourn in Nazareth for thirty years
suggests a similar experience in the life of the Church.   In the
world and yet not of it—a pilgrim and stranger.

they may nourish her. As Elijah was supported in the
wilderness of Sinai (1 Kings xviii. 4) so the Church during her
life on earth is sustained by the heavenly food (John vi. 48–51).
This is only for a comparatively brief time, three and a half
years.

7. And there was war in heaven. This is to explain how
it is that the dragon is on the earth. His former home was in
the heavenly sphere. There it would seem the free will of

8 warred and his angels; and they prevailed not, neither
9 was their place found any more in heaven. And the
great dragon was cast down, the old serpent, he that is
called the Devil and Satan, the deceiver of the whole
world; he was cast down to the earth, and his angels
10 were cast down with him. And I heard a great voice in
heaven, saying, Now is come the salvation, and the
power, and the kingdom of our God, and the authority of
his Christ: for the accuser of our brethren is cast down,
which accuseth them before our God day and night.
11 And they overcame him because of the blood of the
Lamb, and because of the word of their testimony; and
12 they loved not their life even unto death. Therefore
rejoice, O heavens, and ye that dwell in them. Woe for
the earth and for the sea: because the devil is gone
down unto you, having great wrath, knowing that he
hath but a short time.
13   And when the dragon saw that he was cast down to
the earth, he persecuted the woman which brought forth

---

angelic beings was proved and some fell, joining the Arch-
Fiend who with all his is finally driven out of heaven.

9. And the great dragon was cast down. See Luke x. 17-19;
xi. 21 and 22; John xii. 31-33, xvi. 8-11; Heb. ii. 14, 15.
The mystery of the Fall of Satan is very dark. It may mean the
loss of certain spiritual powers by which he was once able to
influence angels. Human beings however, being partly flesh,
partly spirit, may be caught by his wiles. Earth is the only sphere
where he may hope for success. It may be that this casting out
was contemporaneous with the Incarnation, the Passion and the
Ascension. Christ speaks of seeing Satan fall like lightning from
heaven. Luke x. 17-19.

10. the accuser of our brethren is cast down. Accuser
is often, though not here, the translation of the Greek for Devil.
His main work is taking away people's character. Christ's
Intercession gives the answer to Satan's accusation of mankind.

11. they overcame him because of the blood. The conquest
of the Tempter is due to Christ's atoning grace received and
imparted and to courageous determined self-sacrifice which
shrinks not from witnessing to Christ.

13. when the dragon saw...he persecuted. The persecu-

the man *child.*   And there were given to the woman the 14
two wings of the great eagle, that she might fly into the
wilderness unto her place, where she is nourished for a
time, and times, and half a time, from the face of the
serpent.   And the serpent cast out of his mouth after the 15
woman water as a river, that he might cause her to be
carried away by the stream.   And the earth helped the 16
woman, and the earth opened her mouth, and swallowed
up the river which the dragon cast out of his mouth.
And the dragon waxed wroth with the woman, and went 17
away to make war with the rest of her seed, which keep
the commandments of God, and hold the testimony of
Jesus : and he stood upon the sand of the sea.   **13**

---

tions of the Church such as that of Nero are here referred to
their right source.   But Satan's power fails, because by the
spiritual uplift of exaltation that Christ gives her she lives above
it.   See Exod. xix. 4, where Israel's deliverance from Pharaoh
is similarly described.

**14.   there were given to the woman the two wings of the
great eagle.**   The Church escapes from the persecution of Satan
by her faith and love which lift her out of the sphere of the
earth.

**15, 16.   the serpent cast...water...And the earth helped the
woman.**   As Pharaoh hoped the Israelites would be drowned in
the Red Sea, so Satan hoped by a flood of evil to destroy the
Church.   See Ps. xviii. 5 and xxxii. 6 for the metaphor.   The
help of the earth may refer to that sense of justice and fairness,
at least amongst Roman citizens and rulers, e.g. Gallio—which
often prevented mob violence from doing its worst.

**17.   the dragon...went away to make war with the rest of
her seed.**   Finding that he can do but little with the Apostles
and Christian leaders, Satan goes forth to tempt the growing
Gentile part of the Church.

XIII.   1.   he stood upon the sand.   The Dragon stood on the
shore, looking for and expecting his chief ally from the sea,
i.e. the Roman Imperial Power which would come to the
Province of Asia from the sea.

PART II. THE DRAGON CALLS TO HIS AID THE CIVIL
AND RELIGIOUS POWERS OF ROME.

XIII.   In this chapter we have a description of the two powers
that the Dragon now summons to his aid in his endeavours
to overthrow the Church, (1) the Imperial power of Rome,
(2) the Provincial power, civil and religious, of her subject
states.   They are the two beasts, alike in some respects, but
different in others.   The opposition of the Imperial and
Provincial authorities to a religion which was one of love
and for the good of all mankind was a difficulty with St John,
but was now explained.

And I saw a beast coming up out of the sea, having ten
horns and seven heads, and on his horns ten diadems, and
upon his heads names of blasphemy.   And the beast
which I saw was like unto a leopard, and his feet were as
the feet of a bear, and his mouth as the mouth of a lion :
and the dragon gave him his power, and his throne, and
great authority.   And *I saw* one of his heads as though it
had been smitten unto death ; and his death-stroke was

---

ten horns and seven heads.   The ten horns are the ten
Emperors from Augustus to Titus, each horn being crowned ;
the seven heads are those seven to whom divine honours
were paid, on whom were names of blasphemy.   The Emperor
expressed the majesty, wisdom and beneficent power of Rome :
he was in many cases actually represented in different parts of
the Empire as an incarnation of the god worshipped in that
district.   "Domitian delighted...to be idolised as the Divine
Providence in human form : and it is recorded that Caligula,
Domitian and Diocletian were the three Emperors who delighted
to be styled dominus et deus."   (Ramsay, *Church in Roman
Empire*, pp. 191, 275.)

2.   the beast...was like unto a leopard.   See Dan. vii. 2.
This monster of Rome combined the strength, cunning and
brutality of the Babylonian, Median and Persian Empires which
Daniel had seen.

**3.   And I saw one of his heads as though it had been
smitten unto death.**   The head probably represents Nero
(54–64 A.D.) who killed himself when pursued and about whom
there was a rumour in the eastern provinces of the Empire that
he was still alive.   This legend St John makes use of and in
Domitian's persecution sees its truth.   Domitian is Nero come
to life again with all his old hideous cruelty and power.

healed : and the whole earth wondered after the beast ;
and they worshipped the dragon, because he gave his 4
authority unto the beast ; and they worshipped the beast,
saying, Who is like unto the beast? and who is able to
war with him? and there was given to him a mouth 5
speaking great things and blasphemies; and there was
given to him authority to continue forty and two months.
And he opened his mouth for blasphemies against God, to 6
blaspheme his name, and his tabernacle, *even* them that
dwell in the heaven.   And it was given unto him to make 7
war with the saints, and to overcome them : and there
was given to him authority over every tribe and people
and tongue and nation.   And all that dwell on the earth 8
shall worship him, *every one* whose name hath not been
written in the book of life of the Lamb that hath been
slain from the foundation of the world.   If any man hath 9
an ear, let him hear.   If any man *is* for captivity, into 10
captivity he goeth : if any man shall kill with the sword,
with the sword must he be killed.   Here is the patience
and the faith of the saints.

---

4. **they worshipped the dragon.**   The extraordinary power
of Rome aroused enthusiasm for the Pagan religion which was
practically a kind of devil worship.   "As for the direct worship
of the Beast, toward the end of the first century it was already
co-ordinated with the local cults : in Asia the cities vied with one
another for the honour of erecting a temple to Rome and the
Caesars."   Imperial edicts actually began "Our Lord God wills
to be done."   Swete, *The Apocalypse*, p. 161.

5. **authority to continue forty and two months.**   Here
again we have the indeterminate and transient time of 3½ years
mentioned.   The power of the Beast is limited, it will come to
an end.

8. **every one whose name hath not been written.**   All are
ready to pay divine honours to the Roman Emperor except those
who belong to the Church.   They remain loyal to their King.

10. **Here is the patience and the faith.**   The refusal to worship the Beast may mean exile, it may mean execution ; but in any
case it is a test of the loyal devotion of the Saints.

11　And I saw another beast coming up out of the earth ; and he had two horns like unto a lamb, and he spake as 12 a dragon.　And he exerciseth all the authority of the first beast in his sight.　And he maketh the earth and them that dwell therein to worship the first beast, whose death-13 stroke was healed.　And he doeth great signs, that he should even make fire to come down out of heaven upon 14 the earth in the sight of men.　And he deceiveth them that dwell on the earth by reason of the signs which it was given him to do in the sight of the beast ; saying to them that dwell on the earth, that they should make an image to the beast, who hath the stroke of the sword, and lived. 15 And it was given *unto him* to give breath to it, *even* to the image of the beast, that the image of the beast should both speak, and cause that as many as should not worship 16 the image of the beast should be killed.　And he causeth all, the small and the great, and the rich and the poor, and the free and the bond, that there be given them a 17 mark on their right hand, or upon their forehead ; and

---

11. another beast coming up out of the earth.　This other beast, the Provincial Power, comes from the land in which the Apostle is, i.e. from Asia Minor, to meet as it were the Roman Power.

he had two horns, i.e. he had two expressions of power, the civil and religious.　In themselves these seemed to be harmless, " *horns like unto a lamb*," only when urged would they act.　But as a matter of fact they supported the Imperial power, even in the case of the Neronian persecution.　That tyranny excited no such revolt as might have been expected.

13. And he doeth great signs.　Magic, conjuring, ventriloquism were all resorted to in order to support the worship of the Emperors (see 2 Thess. ii. 9).　Images of the Emperors, especially of Nero who was thought to be alive, were set up, and means found by which they seemed to move and speak as though they were alive.

16, 17. he causeth all...that there be given them a mark on their right hand.　Christians were boycotted from the markets and the shops, and devices were resorted to by means of which they were known.　" Knowledge of the name and number of the beast became a sort of password for the Pagans."

that no man should be able to buy or to sell, save he that
hath the mark, *even* the name of the beast or the number
of his name. Here is wisdom. He that hath under- 18
standing, let him count the number of the beast ; for it is
the number of a man : and his number is Six hundred
and sixty and six.

PART III.   EPISODE SHEWING THE SAFETY OF THE REDEEMED.

XIV., XV. After such a terrible description of the power of the
enemy, St John according to his custom (see chapters vii., x.,
xi.) calms his readers by a description of the safety of the
redeemed and the awful judgment that is certain to over-
whelm all those who side with the Dragon and his allies.

And I saw, and behold, the Lamb standing on the **14**
mount Zion, and with him a hundred and forty and four

---

18. **He that hath understanding, let him count the number of the beast,** i.e. " Let the intelligent reader work out the
number of the beast, for Beast though he is, his number **is**
human, i.e. a number such as men use, and his number is 666."
If we are to suppose that St John is using numbers in the same
way throughout the book, then 666 might mean an imperfect
sinful character as 777 would mean a perfect one. But it is at
least strange that the Hebrew numerals, which stand for letters,
should stand for Nero Caesar. " It has been found that if
'Neron Caesar' be written in Hebrew letters the sum of the
letters is 666. This is generally accepted at present, although
to get 666, Caesar has to be written defectively. If spelt 'Nero
Caesar' the sum of the letters is 616, which is the reading of some
MSS." (*One Volume Bible Commentary*, p. 1083.) Supposing
that St John has Domitian in mind as " Nero redivivus," then this
would be a sufficient way for indicating him. He could not
name him because if any Christian were found with a MS bearing
his name this would incriminate him. But why indicate him at
all? Because Christians would be cheered in their persecutions
to know that his tyranny was coming to an end.

XIV. 1. And I saw, and behold, the Lamb. In chapter xii. 3,
"And there was seen...and behold, a great red dragon," here
he saw "and behold, the Lamb." The contrast is remarkable.
Christ, the Protector of His people, is seen in all His gentleness
and self-sacrifice, the centre of the redeemed. Mount Zion

thousand, having his name, and the name of his Father,
2 written on their foreheads. And I heard a voice from
heaven, as the voice of many waters, and as the voice of a
great thunder · and the voice which I heard *was* as *the*
3 *voice* of harpers harping with their harps : and they sing as
it were a new song before the throne, and before the four
living creatures and the elders : and no man could learn
the song save the hundred and forty and four thousand,
even they that had been purchased out of the earth.
4 These are they which were not defiled with women ; for
they are virgins. These *are* they which follow the Lamb

---

where he stands represents "the strong divine foundations of the
new order." The number 144,000 a multiple of 12 signifies the
completeness of the redeemed and the name they bear marks the
important fact that they all know and love the Father. Note
that as the Emperor's followers are sealed with his name, so
Christ's followers are marked with His sign.

2. And I heard a voice. St John not only sees but hears;
and the sound is a combination of beautiful music, with the roar
of tumbling waters and the deep roll of thunder, sweetness and
majesty combined.

3. and they sing...a new song. A song is the joyful
expression of our feelings. The emotions of the redeemed
kindled by the sight of their loved Master as King find one common harmony which is unintelligible to all but those who know
their redemption and how it was won.

4. These are they which were not defiled. The words seem
to imply the unmarried, but it is impossible to confine the 144,000
to such. Marriage was commended by our Lord both in word
and act ("He beautified it by His presence and first miracle")
and is praised by the writer of the Epistle to the Hebrews (Heb.
xiii. 4). St John is not likely to cast any slur upon it. We must
therefore believe that he used these strong words to imply that
high personal purity which may be as characteristic of the
married as of the unmarried state. The word virgin must be
taken metaphorically.

The other marks of the redeemed are obedience, separation
from the world and perfect truthfulness. See Is. lxiii. 8, and
1 Peter ii. 22.

Note the words "purchased...to be the firstfruits" implies a
harvest of some kind that will one day follow. See, for its use
here, Rom. xvi. 5 and 1 Cor. xvi. 15.

whithersoever he goeth. These were purchased from among men, *to be* the firstfruits unto God and unto the Lamb. And in their mouth was found no lie : they are 5 without blemish.

And I saw another angel flying in mid heaven, having 6 an eternal gospel to proclaim unto them that dwell on the earth, and unto every nation and tribe and tongue and people ; and he saith with a great voice, Fear God, and 7 give him glory ; for the hour of his judgement is come : and worship him that made the heaven and the earth and sea and fountains of waters.

And another, a second angel, followed, saying, Fallen, 8 fallen is Babylon the great, which hath made all the nations to drink of the wine of the wrath of her fornication.

And another angel, a third, followed them, saying with 9 a great voice, If any man worshippeth the beast and his image, and receiveth a mark on his forehead, or upon his hand, he also shall drink of the wine of the wrath of God, 10 which is prepared unmixed in the cup of his anger ; and he shall be tormented with fire and brimstone in the

---

6. And I saw another angel. St John not only sees the safety of the redeemed in heaven, but hears the terms on which all may reach it. "The eternal gospel" is the gospel which never changes and which is universal.

7. Fear God, and give him glory. Deep reverence, repentance (see Eccles. xii. 13 and Josh. vii. 19 for the expression "give glory to God") and worship are the unalterable conditions of salvation.

8. Fallen, fallen is Babylon the great. The judgment on Rome is that to which the last verse referred. "There is reason to think that in Jewish and Christian circles Babylon was already an accepted synonym for Rome. Besides 1 Pet. v. 13, where most of the indications point to Rome, see *The Sibylline Oracles*, v., a pre-Christian Book." (Swete, *Apoc.* p. 180.)

9. If any man worshippeth the beast. Judgment would fall not only on Rome but on all those who sympathized or sided with her. This judgment is not necessarily an eternal punishment, but the natural consequence of sin.

presence of the holy angels, and in the presence of the
11 Lamb : and the smoke of their torment goeth up for ever
and ever ; and they have no rest day and night, they
that worship the beast and his image, and whoso receiveth
12 the mark of his name.   Here is the patience of the saints,
they that keep the commandments of God, and the faith
of Jesus.

13   And I heard a voice from heaven saying, Write, Blessed
are the dead which die in the Lord from henceforth : yea,
saith the Spirit, that they may rest from their labours ;
for their works follow with them.

14   And I saw, and behold, a white cloud ; and on the
cloud *I saw* one sitting like unto a son of man, having on
his head a golden crown, and in his hand a sharp sickle.

15 And another angel came out from the temple, crying with
a great voice to him that sat on the cloud, Send forth

---

12. Here is the patience of the saints. In resisting all
temptations to offer incense to the image of the Cæsar, or in any
way to compromise with Rome lay the opportunity to exercise
courageous endurance on the part of those who believed in
Christ.

13. Blessed are the dead. St John knew that not only
exile, his own fate, but death might be the lot of all those who
were loyal to the faith, and he now hears the blessedness of the
martyrs sung in heaven and earth. This consists in the rest they
win and in the fruit of their works which they find in the Paradise whither they go. "Their works follow with them." Nothing
that they have done is lost. The processes, methods, habits
and results of their labours remain.

14. I saw one sitting like unto a son of man. The image
changes. He had seen Christ as a Lamb, he now sees Him as a
human being crowned and about to gather in those who are His.
He had seen Him standing on Mount Zion. He is now seen
sitting on a cloud of judgment.

15. And another angel came out from the temple. "Of
that day and hour...knoweth no man, no, not the angels which
are in heaven, neither the Son but the Father." Mark xiii. 32.
And therefore the message comes out of the Temple, i.e. the
immediate Presence of God, to the Son bidding Him reap.
This harvest is confined to the good, nothing is said about tares.

thy sickle, and reap: for the hour to reap is come; for the harvest of the earth is over-ripe. And he that sat 16 on the cloud cast his sickle upon the earth; and the earth was reaped.

And another angel came out from the temple which is 17 in heaven, he also having a sharp sickle. And another 18 angel came out from the altar, he that hath power over fire; and he called with a great voice to him that had the sharp sickle, saying, Send forth thy sharp sickle, and gather the clusters of the vine of the earth; for her grapes are fully ripe. And the angel cast his sickle into the earth, 19 and gathered the vintage of the earth, and cast it into the winepress, the great *winepress*, of the wrath of God. And the winepress was trodden without the city, and there 20 came out blood from the winepress, even unto the bridles of the horses, as far as a thousand and six hundred furlongs.

And I saw another sign in heaven, great and marvellous, **15** seven angels having seven plagues, *which are* the last, for in them is finished the wrath of God.

---

18. gather the clusters of the vine. Here the judgment of the wicked is described. Christ does not gather them, this is done by the angel of judgment; He came not to condemn but to save.

19. the great winepress of the wrath of God. The grapes are gathered and then cast into the winepress and trodden under foot. The mass of wickedness here judged was so great that the Seer represents it to us by a winepress some two hundred miles long filled with grapes even to a depth of four or five feet, "unto the bridles of the horses." Note the judgment takes place outside the City of God. Sixteen hundred furlongs (400 × 4) may signify the completeness of the judgment.

XV. 1. And I saw another sign. He had seen angels breaking the seven seals, i.e. removing the great obstacles that hinder the furtherance of God's kingdom; he had seen them blowing with the seven trumpets and summoning the world to surrender; he now sees them with seven bowls full of the judgments of God. These judgments are the very last so far as this world is concerned.

2 And I saw as it were a glassy sea mingled with fire ; and them that come victorious from the beast, and from his image, and from the number of his name, standing by the
3 glassy sea, having harps of God. And they sing the song of Moses the servant of God, and the song of the Lamb, saying, Great and marvellous are thy works, O Lord God, the Almighty; righteous and true are thy ways, thou King
4 of the ages. Who shall not fear, O Lord, and glorify thy name? for thou only art holy; for all the nations shall come and worship before thee; for thy righteous acts have been made manifest.

5 And after these things I saw, and the temple of the
6 tabernacle of the testimony in heaven was opened : and there came out from the temple the seven angels that had the seven plagues, arrayed with *precious* stone, pure *and* bright, and girt about their breasts with golden girdles.
7 And one of the four living creatures gave unto the seven angels seven golden bowls full of the wrath of God, who
8 liveth for ever and ever. And the temple was filled with smoke from the glory of God, and from his power ; and none was able to enter into the temple, till the seven plagues of the seven angels should be finished.

---

2. a glassy sea mingled with fire. Before speaking of the last awful judgments he reassures his disciples by bidding them see how safe, happy and honoured the saints are. They stand as Israel stood when their enemies pursued after them, by the sea, i.e. on the sea shore ; or as in the margin, upon the sea ; perhaps referring to Israel being in the midst of the Red Sea, quite safe. In this case the sea was of glass, i.e. expressing the purity of God, but streaked with fire, i.e. marked with His judgments.

3. they sing the song of Moses. This theme, like that of Miriam, is one of redemption. They are safe and recognize the absolute justice of judgments due to His unique Holiness.

6. there came out...the seven angels that had the seven plagues. Note that the punishment of wickedness proceeds from the still quiet shrine of God, where His glory and power abide. God's judgments are not the expression of uncontrolled wrath but of even justice ; and they are mysterious, none being able to understand them (*"none was able to enter into the temple"*) until they are finished.

PART IV. JUDGMENT OF THE ROMAN EMPIRE.

XVI. This chapter recalls chapters vi., viii. and ix. The judgments of God are not now looked upon as the breaking of seals that keep the Book of Human Destiny closed, they are not here regarded as removal of obstacles : nor are they pictured as appeals to the world to surrender, the trumpet blasts of God's wrath ; but as bowls or vials full of God's wrath against sin. They are to the world what the plagues were to Pharaoh and Egypt, designed to lead men to repent and yet failing in their mission. As with Pharaoh there were plagues of frogs, boils, darkness and blood ; so here there are grievous sores, scorching heat, horrible pain ; and as they hardened Pharaoh's heart, so these only stiffen the opposition of the world against Christ.

And I heard a great voice out of the temple, saying to 16 the seven angels, Go ye, and pour out the seven bowls of the wrath of God into the earth.

And the first went, and poured out his bowl into the 2 earth ; and it became a noisome and grievous sore upon the men which had the mark of the beast, and which worshipped his image.

And the second poured out his bowl into the sea ; and 3 it became blood as of a dead man ; and every living soul died, *even* the things that were in the sea.

And the third poured out his bowl into the rivers and 4 the fountains of the waters ; and it became blood. And I 5

XVI. 2. it became a noisome and grievous sore. This is the effect of sin on those who are worldly-minded, it brings its own punishment.

3. and it became blood. The glorious sea which refreshes and purifies becomes to the wicked a source of corruption. God's gifts for those who sin become curses.

4. the third poured out his bowl into the rivers and the fountains. Here again the fresh cool springs become infectious. Perhaps it refers to the springs of literature and art, all of which at the time when St John wrote became poisonous. They had the effect of bringing about terrible depression which led to suicide, at this time extremely common.

heard the angel of the waters saying, Righteous art thou,
which art and which wast, thou Holy One, because thou
didst thus judge : for they poured out the blood of saints
and prophets, and blood hast thou given them to drink :
they are worthy. And I heard the altar saying, Yea,
O Lord God, the Almighty, true and righteous are thy
judgements.

And the fourth poured out his bowl upon the sun ; and
it was given unto it to scorch men with fire. And men
were scorched with great heat : and they blasphemed the
name of the God which hath the power over these plagues ;
and they repented not to give him glory.

And the fifth poured out his bowl upon the throne of
the beast ; and his kingdom was darkened ; and they
gnawed their tongues for pain, and they blasphemed the
God of heaven because of their pains and their sores ; and
they repented not of their works.

And the sixth poured out his bowl upon the great river,
the *river* Euphrates ; and the water thereof was dried up,

---

5. Righteous art thou. This dark gloomy love of death
was felt by the saints to be a natural judgment on those who
"had poured out the blood of saints and prophets."

8. it was given unto it to scorch men. The sun with its
cheering light and warmth is felt by the wicked to be an instrument of pain and death. When looked at in the wrong way,
that which illuminates and gives life, such as the glorious gospel
of God, injures. Christ Himself the Sun of Righteousness was
more hated during his lifetime by the world than any one before
or since; and His blessed teaching was followed by hateful
blasphemy rather than repentance.

10. his kingdom was darkened. The brilliancy of the
world suffered eclipse. Nero's reign was an awful time of moral
and spiritual darkness, in spite of Seneca.

**12. the sixth poured out his bowl upon...the river
Euphrates.** The Euphrates stands for that wall of civilization
which kept off from the Roman Empire the Eastern hordes that
threatened it. Order and justice made the Roman provincial
cities strong bulwarks. But now civilization gives way. And
the Devil, the Empire and paganism produce the foulest and
blackest sins, shaming even the low public standard of morals.

that the way might be made ready for the kings that *come*
from the sunrising.   And I saw *coming* out of the mouth 13
of the dragon, and out of the mouth of the beast, and out
of the mouth of the false prophet, three unclean spirits, as
it were frogs : for they are spirits of devils, working signs ; 14
which go forth unto the kings of the whole world, to
gather them together unto the war of the great day of
God, the Almighty. (Behold, I come as a thief.   Blessed 15
is he that watcheth, and keepeth his garments, lest he
walk naked, and they see his shame.)   And they gathered 16
them together into the place which is called in Hebrew
Har-Magedon.

And the seventh poured out his bowl upon the air ; and 17
there came forth a great voice out of the temple, from the
throne, saying, It is done : and there were lightnings, 18
and voices, and thunders ; and there was a great earthquake, such as was not since there were men upon the
earth, so great an earthquake, so mighty.   And the great 19
city was divided into three parts, and the cities of the

And this was specially seen in the imperial court which cared
nothing for morality and was seized with a fanatical passion for
war. See *v.* 14.

15. lest he walk naked, and they see his shame. Here the
Seer interposes a warning based on the silence of our Lord's
coming.   Death will be a revelation of character, shameful to
those who are not in Christ.   There is also an encouragement to
watch.   Any guard of the Temple found asleep had his garments
burnt ; so here blessed is he that *keepeth* his garments ; it is a
sign of his watchfulness.   Edersheim, *The Temple, its Ministry
and Services*, p. 120.

16. the place which is called…Har-Magedon. Megiddo
was the great battlefield of Palestine, partly because it was the
only level plain where horses and chariots could be used with any
advantage (see Judg. v. 19 ; 2 Kings ix. 27 and 2 Kings xxiii.
29).   Har-Megiddo or Mt Megiddo is difficult, as there is no
mountain of that name, but quite possibly, as Dr Swete suggests,
St John has Ezek. xxxix. 2 in his mind, "I am against thee, O
Gog…and will bring thee upon the mountains of Israel" (Rev.
xx. 8), a passage justified in this connection by the spurs of
Mt Carmel which abut the plain.

19. And the great city was divided into three parts. At

nations fell: and Babylon the great was remembered in
the sight of God, to give unto her the cup of the wine of
20 the fierceness of his wrath. And every island fled away,
21 and the mountains were not found. And great hail, *every
stone* about the weight of a talent, cometh down out of
heaven upon men: and men blasphemed God because of
the plague of the hail ; for the plague thereof is exceeding
great.

PART V. JUDGMENT OF ROME.

XVII. 1—XIX. 10. This next division of the book is wholly
concerned with the judgment on Rome. She was the "fons
et origo" of all the persecutions of Christianity and of all
the hateful sins and immoralities that desolated the Empire.
Mighty and proud as this Western Babylon was, it was a
special gratification to the Apostle to see at last the heavy
judgment of God descend upon her. And this destruction
of the world's great city prepared the way for the vision of
God's great city. The one stands against the other.

17 And there came one of the seven angels that had the
seven bowls, and spake with me, saying, Come hither, I
will shew thee the judgement of the great harlot that
2 sitteth upon many waters ; with whom the kings of the
earth committed fornication, and they that dwell in the
earth were made drunken with the wine of her fornication.
3 And he carried me away in the Spirit into a wilderness:
and I saw a woman sitting upon a scarlet-coloured beast,

---

last the judgments strike Rome, the centre of the life of the
Empire. The city is split into three and its partial ruin is
emphasized by the fall of several provincial cities. The judgment
on Rome was specially severe, owing to its wickedness.

XVII. 1. the great harlot that sitteth upon many waters.
The language is figurative, borrowed from Jeremiah's description
of Babylon (li. 13). The waters were the peoples, nations and
tongues scattered throughout the Empire (see xvii. 15).

3. he carried me away in the Spirit into a wilderness. A
desert is the fitting place from which he can see the awful
destruction of Jerusalem, as a mountain is the fitting place
whence he can see the City of God (xxi. 10).

I saw a woman.... Rome is pictured as a bad woman riding

full of names of blasphemy, having seven heads and ten
horns. And the woman was arrayed in purple and scarlet, 4
and decked with gold and precious stone and pearls, having
in her hand a golden cup full of abominations, even the
unclean things of her fornication, and upon her forehead 5
a name written, MYSTERY, BABYLON THE GREAT, THE
MOTHER OF THE HARLOTS AND OF THE ABOMINATIONS
OF THE EARTH. And I saw the woman drunken with the 6
blood of the saints, and with the blood of the martyrs of
Jesus. And when I saw her, I wondered with a great
wonder. And the angel said unto me, Wherefore didst 7
thou wonder? I will tell thee the mystery of the woman,
and of the beast that carrieth her, which hath the seven
heads and the ten horns. The beast that thou sawest 8
was, and is not ; and is about to come up out of the abyss,

---

upon a scarlet-coloured Beast, full of the spirit of independence
of God. The Beast is the Empire or great world-power of
which Rome was Mistress. The seven heads and ten horns are
explained later.

5. upon her forehead a name written, Mystery. i.e. "My
inner meaning is that I represent a great city which is to the
world of to-day what Babylon was centuries ago."

6. I saw the woman drunken with the blood of the saints.
The terrible Neronian persecution quite justified this strong
language.

I wondered with a great wonder. Because he had expected
something so different. He had been told that he would see
the judgment of the great whore, and he sees her apparently
triumphant. This makes the interpretation difficult and he wel-
comes the guidance of the angel who is to explain the meaning
of the mystery.

8. The beast that thou sawest was, and is not. That is, it
once lived but now lives no more and it will reappear out of the
abyss into which it has been cast and then return to the pit of
destruction to which it belongs. This resurrection from the
pit will excite universal astonishment. To understand this we
must remember that the death of Nero, sudden and to some
extent secret, started a rumour that he had not died and would
return one day from the East. St John takes hold of this
rumour and justifies it by the reign of the wicked Domitian so
active in his persecution of the Christians. He is the "Nero

and to go into perdition. And they that dwell on the earth shall wonder, *they* whose name hath not been written in the book of life from the foundation of the world, when they behold the beast, how that he was, and is not, and
9 shall come. Here is the mind which hath wisdom. The seven heads are seven mountains, on which the woman
10 sitteth : and they are seven kings ; the five are fallen, the one is, the other is not yet come ; and when he cometh,
11 he must continue a little while. And the beast that was, and is not, is himself also an eighth, and is of the seven ;
12 and he goeth into perdition. And the ten horns that thou sawest are ten kings, which have received no kingdom as yet ; but they receive authority as kings, with the beast,
13 for one hour. These have one mind, and they give their

---

redivivus." All but the Christians are astonished at the vitality of an Empire that can reproduce such a fiend so soon after his death.

9, 10. The seven heads are seven mountains. Rome represents the head of the Beast, and Rome was expressed in seven Emperor Kings : Augustus, Tiberius, Caligula, Claudius, Nero, Vespasian and Titus (the three Emperors Galba, Otho, Vitellius, who reigned barely a year between them, are omitted). Out of these seven, five were already dead, Vespasian being alive when the first edition of the Apocalypse was written and Titus being still to come. Domitian who succeeded Titus was the eighth. It may be that *v.* 11 was added and the previous verse modified in a second edition of the book. But the whole passage is admittedly difficult, though the interpretation seems better than that which makes the five kingdoms mean the kingdoms of Egypt, Assyria, Babylon, Persia, Greece, the sixth which was still existing Rome, the seventh a power not yet known and the eighth Anti-Christ. Such an explanation seems to have no relation to the context.

12. the ten horns...are ten kings. These are the still unborn forces of the Empire, they will however possess quasi-Imperial power, "*they give their power unto the beast*," but will only last for a comparatively short time. The number ten is not to be taken literally but as indicating any number ; it does not indicate perfection like seven, though definiteness is probably included in it. It is a known number but " with the exact figure uncertain."

13. These have one mind. They will all be one in their

power and authority unto the beast. These shall war 14
against the Lamb, and the Lamb shall overcome them,
for he is Lord of lords, and King of kings ; and they *also
shall overcome* that are with him, called and chosen and
faithful. And he saith unto me, The waters which thou 15
sawest, where the harlot sitteth, are peoples, and multi-
tudes, and nations, and tongues. And the ten horns which 16
thou sawest, and the beast, these shall hate the harlot, and
shall make her desolate and naked, and shall eat her flesh,
and shall burn her utterly with fire. For God did put in 17
their hearts to do his mind, and to come to one mind, and
to give their kingdom unto the beast, until the words of
God should be accomplished. And the woman whom 18
thou sawest is the great city, which reigneth over the kings
of the earth.

After these things I saw another angel coming down **18**
out of heaven, having great authority ; and the earth was
lightened with his glory. And he cried with a mighty 2
voice, saying, Fallen, fallen is Babylon the great, and is
become a habitation of devils, and a hold of every unclean
spirit, and a hold of every unclean and hateful bird. For 3

---

opposition to Christianity. So far they "give their power and
authority unto the beast."

16. **these shall hate the harlot.** Though united in their
hatred to Christianity, they have no love for Rome ; on the con-
trary their wish is to destroy her. And this they will be able to
do because of the spirit of unity which God inspires them with
for His own purposes.

XVIII. 1. another angel...having great authority. Angels
are not all alike, some have less, some have more authority.
The high authority of this one is seen by the light which his
figure throws across the earth.

2. **Fallen, fallen is Babylon.** Not through outward judgment
but inner hidden decay. Possessed by foul spirits, " *a habitation
of devils*," and bereft of all good, she was sure to tumble into ruin.
The sack of Rome took place in 410 by Alaric, the Goth, again
in 455 by Genseric, the Vandal, and again in 476 by Odoacer, the
Goth, when the great Empire came to an end.

by the wine of the wrath of her fornication all the nations
are fallen ; and the kings of the earth committed fornication with her, and the merchants of the earth waxed rich
by the power of her wantonness.

4   And I heard another voice from heaven, saying, Come
forth, my people, out of her, that ye have no fellowship
5 with her sins, and that ye receive not of her plagues : for
her sins have reached even unto heaven, and God hath
6 remembered her iniquities.   Render unto her even as she
rendered, and double *unto her* the double according to
her works : in the cup which she mingled, mingle unto
7 her double.   How much soever she glorified herself, and
waxed wanton, so much give her of torment and mourning : for she saith in her heart, I sit a queen, and am no
8 widow, and shall in no wise see mourning.   Therefore in
one day shall her plagues come, death, and mourning,
and famine ; and she shall be utterly burned with fire ;
9 for strong is the Lord God which judged her.   And the
kings of the earth, who committed fornication and lived
wantonly with her, shall weep and wail over her, when
10 they look upon the smoke of her burning, standing afar
off for the fear of her torment, saying, Woe, woe, the
great city, Babylon, the strong city ! for in one hour is

---

3. by the wine of the wrath of her fornication.   This is a
very powerful metaphor for describing the maddening effect of
her wickedness.   The nations who were under her influence
became stupefied by all that they heard and saw and were
stimulated to every conceivable cruelty.

4.   Come forth, my people.   This is a strong appeal to the
Christians not so much perhaps to abandon the city as to live
separate from her life, to have "no fellowship with her sins"; see
2 Cor. vi. 14 and 1 Tim. v. 22.

6. Render unto her even as she rendered.   The sense of
justice outraged as it has been by the wicked persecutions that
had taken place cries out for satisfaction.   This is the more urgent
owing to the calm self-complacency which Rome expresses.   Her
long reign led her to suppose that nothing could ever happen to
her.

thy judgement come. And the merchants of the earth 11
weep and mourn over her, for no man buyeth their merchandise any more; merchandise of gold, and silver, and 12
precious stone, and pearls, and fine linen, and purple, and
silk, and scarlet; and all thyine wood, and every vessel
of ivory, and every vessel made of most precious wood,
and of brass, and iron, and marble; and cinnamon, and 13
spice, and incense, and ointment, and frankincense, and
wine, and oil, and fine flour, and wheat, and cattle, and
sheep; and *merchandise* of horses and chariots and
slaves; and souls of men. And the fruits which thy 14
soul lusted after are gone from thee, and all things that
were dainty and sumptuous are perished from thee, and
men shall find them no more at all. The merchants of 15
these things, who were made rich by her, shall stand afar
off for the fear of her torment, weeping and mourning;
saying, Woe, woe, the great city, she that was arrayed in 16
fine linen and purple and scarlet, and decked with gold
and precious stone and pearl! for in one hour so great 17

**11. And the merchants of the earth weep and mourn over
her.** If London perished we should be at once face to face
with a commercial crisis which would affect the whole world.
So too the fall of Rome affected the business of the whole
Empire. She was the great purchaser from all the markets of
the East and bought all they offered even to the bodies and
souls of men. Gibbon (*Decline and Fall*, I. Cap. 2) writes "the
most remote countries of the ancient world were ransacked to
supply the pomp and delicacy of Rome....The return of the fleet
was fixed to the months of December or January and as soon as
their rich cargo had been transplanted on the backs of camels
from the Red Sea to the Nile and had descended that river as far
as Alexandria, it was poured without delay into the capital of the
Empire."

13. horses and chariots and slaves and souls of men.
"The climax of wicked worldliness is reached in this last; it
gives the finishing touch to the picture of society wholly engrossed
in pleasure and indolence and selfishness which lays every market
under tribute to add to its luxuriousness and sacrifices not only
the happiness but the lives and liberties of their fellow creatures
to their own enjoyment" (Boyd Carpenter, *The Revelation*).

riches is made desolate. And every shipmaster, and every one that saileth any whither, and mariners, and as many 18 as gain their living by sea, stood afar off, and cried out as they looked upon the smoke of her burning, saying, What 19 *city* is like the great city? And they cast dust on their heads, and cried, weeping and mourning, saying, Woe, woe, the great city, wherein were made rich all that had their ships in the sea by reason of her costliness! for in 20 one hour is she made desolate. Rejoice over her, thou heaven, and ye saints, and ye apostles, and ye prophets; for God hath judged your judgement on her.

21 And a strong angel took up a stone as it were a great millstone, and cast it into the sea, saying, Thus with a mighty fall shall Babylon, the great city, be cast down, 22 and shall be found no more at all. And the voice of harpers and minstrels and flute-players and trumpeters shall be heard no more at all in thee; and no craftsman, of whatsoever craft, shall be found any more at all in thee; and the voice of a millstone shall be heard no more 23 at all in thee; and the light of a lamp shall shine no more at all in thee; and the voice of the bridegroom and of the bride shall be heard no more at all in thee: for thy merchants were the princes of the earth; for with thy 24 sorcery were all the nations deceived. And in her was

---

20. Rejoice over her The Divine Voice of Justice appeals to those whose cause had been ridiculed and whose leaders had been destroyed to rejoice in the infliction of deserved punishment.

21. Thus with a mighty fall shall Babylon. As Babylon had disappeared, so too Rome shall disappear, and so in some three hundred years after the death of St John, she did. The sack of Rome under Alaric and specially some fifty years later under Genseric, when for fourteen successive days Rome was pillaged, brought the great city to the verge of ruin which was completed by Odoacer before the end of the fifth century.

23. The light of a lamp shall shine no more. Rome set in darkness and silence—not even a sound of joy could be anywhere heard.

found the blood of prophets and of saints, and of all that
have been slain upon the earth.

XIX. 1–10. The joy in Heaven. There is no note here of
malicious selfish triumph. The spiritual world rejoices at
the fall of Rome, partly because it means the fall of wickedness and the diminution of the awful power of evil which
lay in the guilty city, and partly because justice was satisfied.
For a long time evil had triumphed, now at last it was
overthrown.

After these things I heard as it were a great voice of a **19**
great multitude in heaven, saying, Hallelujah; Salvation,
and glory, and power, belong to our God : for true and **2**
righteous are his judgements ; for he hath judged the
great harlot, which did corrupt the earth with her fornication, and he hath avenged the blood of his servants at
her hand.   And a second time they say, Hallelujah.   And **3**
her smoke goeth up for ever and ever.   And the four and **4**
twenty elders and the four living creatures fell down and
worshipped God that sitteth on the throne, saying, Amen ;
Hallelujah.   And a voice came forth from the throne, **5**
saying, Give praise to our God, all ye his servants, ye that
fear him, the small and the great.   And I heard as it **6**
were the voice of a great multitude, and as the voice of
many waters, and as the voice of mighty thunders, saying,
Hallelujah : for the Lord our God, the Almighty, reigneth.
Let us rejoice and be exceeding glad, and let us give the **7**
glory unto him : for the marriage of the Lamb is come,

XIX. 3. And a second time they say, Hallelujah. The out-
burst of joy cannot be contained in one expression. Again and
again the shout of triumph was raised. For the force of iteration
see Ps. lxii. 11, and Job xxxiii. 14.

**4. And the four and twenty elders and the four living
creatures fell down.** Nature as well as the Church rejoiced at
this overthrow of evil. It is good to remember that Repentance
as well as Judgment causes joy in heaven, Luke xv. 7.

**7. Let us rejoice and be exceeding glad...for the marriage
of the Lamb is come.** Here is another reason for joy. In one
sense the union between the Son of God and Human Nature

8 and his wife hath made herself ready. And it was given
unto her that she should array herself in fine linen, bright
and pure : for the fine linen is the righteous acts of the
9 saints. And he saith unto me, Write, Blessed are they
which are bidden to the marriage supper of the Lamb.
And he saith unto me, These are true words of God.
10 And I fell down before his feet to worship him. And he
saith unto me, See thou do it not : I am a fellow-servant
with thee and with thy brethren that hold the testimony
of Jesus : worship God : for the testimony of Jesus is the
spirit of prophecy.

---

was effected on Christmas day and that is the wedding day of the
Church. But the effects of this union are so secret and hidden
that it is open for some to say that the Incarnation never took
place. But one day the Universe will see the results of the
Incarnation in the glory of countless human beings who have
responded to the power of grace. It is "given to her to array
herself in fine linen, bright and pure," and "the fine linen is the
righteous acts of the saints." The Church will be seen as the
most beautiful and perfect society of which the world has ever
dreamed. Every virtue and grace will be hers and all will be
recognized as due to Christ her head. The marriage of Christ
with her then represents the most wonderful expression of outer
and inner beauty of glory as the dress of moral perfection. But
see Matt. xxii. 1-14.

9. These are true words of God. These words may refer to
the essential veracity of the whole series of revelations now
completed (xvii. 1–xix. 9) or to the reality of the blessedness
which all who are bidden to the marriage supper will experience.

10. I fell down before his feet. See xxii. 8 and note that
an ancient writer remarks that a tendency to angel worship
lingered long in Asia Minor. Perhaps seeing the danger St John
felt the more ready to give his own experience.

the testimony of Jesus is the spirit of prophecy. The
angel explains that he is only the fellow-servant of St John and
of those who witness to Jesus, he has no superior position ; and
then he describes who they are who bear witness to Jesus—they
are the prophets, for to witness to Jesus is the work of the
prophets. Or it may mean that the angel here explains that he
deserves no worship, for he is engaged in the same work that
St John and all who witness to Christ have, for bearing witness
to Christ is the very essential characteristic of prophesying, his
own work.

PART VI. OVERTHROW OF PAGANISM.

XIX. 11–21. St John now sees a new revelation. The destruction of the city of Rome has been seen, but nothing has
been said about the power of the Empire or the power of
Paganism; it is the overthrow of these that St John now
sees.

And I saw the heaven opened; and behold, a white 11
horse, and he that sat thereon, called Faithful and True;
and in righteousness he doth judge and make war. And 12
his eyes *are* a flame of fire, and upon his head *are* many
diadems; and he hath a name written, which no one
knoweth but he himself. And he *is* arrayed in a garment 13
sprinkled with blood: and his name is called The Word
of God. And the armies which are in heaven followed 14
him upon white horses, clothed in fine linen, white *and*

---

11. and behold, a white horse. A vision of the conquering
Christ Who rides at the head of His army. This is the third great
picture of Christ. He has been seen as the Son of Man, the
great High Priest ministering to and warning His Church, i. 13:
also as the strong Son of God, the Lion of the tribe of Judah,
v. 5, Who guides the history and progress of the world, v. 6, and
now He is seen as the Captain of a victorious host.

12. a name written, which no one knoweth but he himself.
We know Christ as Saviour, King, High Priest and Judge, but
we do not know all. There is yet another character, it may be
that in which He stands to the other worlds that make up the
Universe.

13. a garment sprinkled with blood. His conquest implies
suffering, that is inevitable, but He does not shrink from it. He
Himself enters into the very thick of the fight.

his name is called The Word of God. One of the connections
with the Gospel, meaning that Christ is the final revelation of
God.

14. And the armies which are in heaven. These are the
angelic hosts. The phrase "armies or hosts of heaven" is constantly used either for the ordered ranks of the heavenly bodies
or the angelic bodyguard of the throne of God. Comp. the title
"Lord God of Sabaoth." (See Driver, Art. "Hosts of Heaven"
in Hastings' *B. D.*) They are clothed in fine linen, for this
expresses their purity.

15 pure. And out of his mouth proceedeth a sharp sword, that with it he should smite the nations : and he shall rule them with a rod of iron : and he treadeth the wine-press of the fierceness of the wrath of Almighty God.

16 And he hath on his garment and on his thigh a name written, KING OF KINGS, AND LORD OF LORDS.

17 And I saw an angel standing in the sun ; and he cried with a loud voice, saying to all the birds that fly in mid heaven, Come *and* be gathered together unto the great

18 supper of God ; that ye may eat the flesh of kings, and the flesh of captains, and the flesh of mighty men, and the flesh of horses and of them that sit thereon, and the flesh of all men, both free and bond, and small and great.

19 And I saw the beast, and the kings of the earth, and their armies, gathered together to make war against him

20 that sat upon the horse, and against his army. And the beast was taken, and with him the false prophet that wrought the signs in his sight, wherewith he deceived

---

15. he treadeth the winepress of the fierceness. See Is. lxiii. 1, to which allusion is made. Christ as Righteousness and pure Justice necessarily treads all sin, injustice, impurity, cruelty under His feet. There is no thought here of selfish vengeance, but only of the triumph of Right.

16. he hath on his garment. This title of Sovereignty is read by everyone, for it is on His robe and on that part of it which covers the thigh, so that all can see it.

17. I saw an angel standing in the sun. The angel is seen standing in that part of the heaven whence he can best summon those winged scavengers who can clear the battlefield of the hosts of the slain who have been deteated in the great victory of the conquering Christ. What is specially intended by this it is diffi-cult to know. Every moral victory leaves a good deal to be cleared up and these are they who do it. See Matt. xxiv. 28 and Ezek. xxxix. 17.

20. And the beast was taken, and with him the false prophet. With the fall of Rome there came the fall of all the provincial organizations which had taken such an active part in the persecutions of the Christians, and also the overthrow of the lying and immoral priesthood with all the magical powers that found play there.

them that had received the mark of the beast, and them
that worshipped his image : they twain were cast alive
into the lake of fire that burneth with brimstone : and 21
the rest were killed with the sword of him that sat upon
the horse, *even the sword* which came forth out of his
mouth : and all the birds were filled with their flesh.

PART VII. OVERTHROW OF THE DRAGON.

XX. Rome is destroyed, Paganism has gone, but what about the
Arch-Fiend? Will he be allowed to find a new field for his
wicked restless energy? In this chapter we see the answer.
Satan is first bound and then cast into the lake of fire.

And I saw an angel coming down out of heaven, having **20**
the key of the abyss and a great chain in his hand.   And 2
he laid hold on the dragon, the old serpent, which is the
Devil and Satan, and bound him for a thousand years,
and cast him into the abyss, and shut *it*, and sealed *it* 3
over him, that he should deceive the nations no more,
until the thousand years should be finished : after this he
must be loosed for a little time.

XX. 1. the key of the abyss. Of course the language here is
only figurative. It pictures a place or state where the Evil One
and his hosts are under restraint. As Dr Swete writes, the
abyss, with its black and bottomless depths, forms an antithesis
to the open shallow pool of fire (xix. 20).

2. the old serpent, which is the Devil. Three names here
give different aspects of the great enemy of mankind. He has
the cunning of a snake, the malice of a constant slanderer (Devil),
and the hatred of a persistent enemy (Satan).

for a thousand years. There is of course no idea here of
mentioning a definite period of ten centuries. Numbers always
in this book stand for ideas and the idea here is that for a long
limited time Satan is a prisoner. It is to be noted that the abyss
where he is confined is an object of dread to evil spirits (Lk. viii.
31). Possibly it represents nothingness and there is no pain to
an evil being, whether man or spirit, so great as that of being
obliged to do nothing except think of the awful wickedness of
which he has been the instrument.

3. after this he must be loosed. Constantly through the New
Testament there are warnings of a great outbreak of evil before
the very end.

4   And I saw thrones, and they sat upon them, and judgement was given unto them : and *I saw* the souls of them
that had been beheaded for the testimony of Jesus, and
for the word of God, and such as worshipped not the beast,
neither his image, and received not the mark upon their
forehead and upon their hand ; and they lived, and reigned
5 with Christ a thousand years.   The rest of the dead lived
not until the thousand years should be finished.   This is
6 the first resurrection.   Blessed and holy is he that hath
part in the first resurrection : over these the second death
hath no power ; but they shall be priests of God and of
Christ, and shall reign with him a thousand years.

---

4. And I saw thrones, and they sat upon them. This represents the other side of the picture.   On the one hand there is
the abyss in which Satan and his host are confined and on the
other there are thrones on which the Saints reign.   St John sees
the powerful influence which martyrs and confessors exercise
upon the earth.   They are not asleep but reigning and ruling.
The history of the world is probably more helped by those who
have won their thrones than by living saints.   The latter work
but the former reign.

5.   The rest of the dead lived not. This certainly seems to
mean that only those who have bravely confessed Christ and
refused to live to the world attain fulness of life after death.   The
rest may have a dreamlike existence, but it is only a shadow life
and they must wait till the second coming of Christ.

This is the first resurrection. This does not imply a resurrection body, but rather a resurrection in the spirit, i.e. a
full consciousness of what Christ is doing, a conscious share in
His blessed work of ruling and guiding.   St John feels that this
high privilege means great happiness.

6.   over these the second death hath no power. Those who
share the reign of Christ need have no fear of the second death
which follows Christ's judgment.   They look on with joy to the
resurrection of the body.   It is to be noted that St John says he
saw "the souls of them that had been beheaded," not the bodies,
for these were not yet given them.

**they shall be priests of God...and shall reign with him a
thousand years.** The reign with Christ is evidently through
their priesthood, i.e. through the offering of their lives and the
intercession that is bound up with it.   The influence of the
Saints is incalculable, not only in the example of their lives and

And when the thousand years are finished, Satan shall 7 be loosed out of his prison, and shall come forth to 8 deceive the nations which are in the four corners of the earth, Gog and Magog, to gather them together to the war : the number of whom is as the sand of the sea. And they went up over the breadth of the earth, and 9 compassed the camp of the saints about, and the beloved city : and fire came down out of heaven, and devoured them. And the devil that deceived them was cast into the 10 lake of fire and brimstone, where are also the beast and the false prophet ; and they shall be tormented day and night for ever and ever.

And I saw a great white throne, and him that sat upon 11

---

the power of their words, which have been handed on from generation to generation and are slowly moulding public opinion, but through their prayers. Being conscious and very near to God they naturally carry on their life of prayer, only with more effectiveness. The "thousand years" is a name for a long and yet limited time ; cp. xi. 3 ff., where the time of persecution is noted as 1260 days; here where the triumph of the Church is indicated it is for 1000 years.

7. And when the thousand years are finished, Satan shall be loosed. Just before the return of Christ to judge there will be a great outbreak of wickedness. Our Lord speaks of the condition of Christianity then as of one of almost total unbelief. See Luke xviii. 8. Though civilization will have no doubt made great progress, yet it will be accompanied by increasing materialism and corresponding doubt in the spiritual world. A final conflict between faith and unbelief is therefore certain and Satan has liberty in the end to hasten it forward.

8. Gog and Magog are simply names for the enemies of Christ (see Ezek. xxxviii. 14 and foll.), being so used not only in Holy Scripture but also in Rabbinical writings (see Dr Swete's note here). They stand for a huge host who attack the Church but fail and are finally consumed by fire.

10. and they shall be tormented day and night. This is the fate of the great leaders of the rebellion against God. There is nothing to shew that their punishment is a torture devised by God. The "lake of fire and brimstone" may be to them their "own place" (see Acts i. 25), the only place where they could be.

Their torment is eternal because their sin is eternal : if the latter were got rid of, the former would disappear.

it, from whose face the earth and the heaven fled away;
12 and there was found no place for them.   And I saw the
dead, the great and the small, standing before the throne ;
and books were opened : and another book was opened,
which is *the book* of life : and the dead were judged out of
the things which were written in the books, according to
13 their works.   And the sea gave up the dead which were
in it ; and death and Hades gave up the dead which were
in them : and they were judged every man according to
14 their works.   And death and Hades were cast into the
lake of fire.   This is the second death, *even* the lake of
15 fire.   And if any was not found written in the book of life,
he was cast into the lake of fire.

PART VIII.   THE THIRD VISION.   THE NEW JERUSALEM.

XXI.   Now that heaven and earth are passed away, Death and
Hades destroyed, Satan and all who belong to him cast into
the lake of fire, we desire to know what takes their place,
where do the righteous dwell?   This St John answers in the
wonderful vision of the holy city.   Note that countless as
the righteous are in number, they dwell in a city, not in
a land.   Fellowship and activity are emphasized rather than
personal comfort.   The description is of course figurative,
and no picture drawn on St John's lines would be anything
but grotesque.

---

11.   and there was found no place for them.   The present
external order will be changed (see Ps. cii. 27, civ. 29, 30 and
Mark xiii. 31 ; 2 Pet. iii. 10).   Our Lord hints that in the
Universe another place is being prepared for the righteous, as
this earth was prepared for mankind (John xiv. 2).

12.   I saw the dead...standing.   A figure of speech to describe
the universal character of the judgment.   The "books opened"
are the revelations of human character which are made with an
unerring hand.   Perfect justice is done to everyone, the reward being
meted out according to actions.   The book of life is that which
contains the names of all those who belong to the Life, i.e. to Christ.

14.   And death and Hades were cast into the lake of fire.
All that death means and all that the disembodied state means
disappear in the lake of fire, i.e. they give way to it.   It takes
their place and is called "the second death" because it is a death
that follows the dissolution of body and soul as something
further.   No words can describe the horror of it, no mind can
imagine its misery.

And I saw a new heaven and a new earth : for the first **21**
heaven and the first earth are passed away ; and the sea
is no more. And I saw the holy city, new Jerusalem, **2**
coming down out of heaven from God, made ready as a
bride adorned for her husband. And I heard a great **3**
voice out of the throne saying, Behold, the tabernacle of
God is with men, and he shall dwell with them, and they
shall be his peoples, and God himself shall be with them,
and be their God : and he shall wipe away every tear from
their eyes ; and death shall be no more ; neither shall **4**
there be mourning, nor crying, nor pain, any more : the

XXI. 1. a new heaven and a new earth. The setting of the
heavenly city will not be on this earth but in new surroundings.
The present world will have vanished—burnt up as St Peter
predicts—and the new resurrection life will be begun on a new
earth.

the sea is no more. The sea is symbolical of separation,
unrest, destruction, and as none of these elements can find any
place in "the restoration of all things" (Acts iii. 21), there is no
place found for the sea.

2. thè holy city. St John does not see the metropolis of
the new earth being built up by famous architects, but coming
down ready made from heaven—from God—Who is the real
builder (Heb. xi. 10). The words describe the Church here
as a city with all the varied life and interest that characterize a
city.

made ready as a bride. The Church in her resurrection life
is glorious, "without any blemish," ready for that full fellowship
with her Lord which was not possible here.

3. Behold, the tabernacle of God is with men. We think of
that time when the Word was made flesh and "tabernacled"
amongst us (John i. 14). But that union was unseen and but
little known by any except the faithful. Now there is some outward visible expression of the glory of this union with mankind.
She is all glorious within with the graces of her Redeemer (Ps.
xlv. ; 1 Pet. iii. 3), and has a wonderful splendour.

they shall be his peoples. They always have been but now
their relation to Him is expressed by their brightness and joyous-
ness, by their power over death which is no longer able to touch
them.

4. the first things. The first dispensation, marked by pain,
grief and death, has now gone for ever.

5 first things are passed away. And he that sitteth on the
throne said, Behold, I make all things new. And he saith,
6 Write : for these words are faithful and true. And he said
unto me, They are come to pass. I am the Alpha and the
Omega, the beginning and the end. I will give unto
7 him that is athirst of the fountain of the water of life
freely. He that overcometh shall inherit these things ;
8 and I will be his God, and he shall be my son. But
for the fearful, and unbelieving, and abominable, and
murderers, and fornicators, and sorcerers, and idolaters,

---

5. And he that sitteth on the throne. God now speaks to
emphasize what the Seer has seen. He declares that He makes
all things new, i.e. that the whole creation has a fresh appearance
and fresh life. Perhaps the difference does not so much consist
in everything being different as in everything being quite fresh
and young.

these words are faithful. Such a promise is absolutely to
be relied on, nay more, it has actually come to pass. The
regeneration is not in the future, it has taken place, though the
outward visible form of its expression is still hidden. And this
because of the relation of the Church to Christ. Christ is the
End as well as the Beginning and therefore necessarily all in
Him is accomplished, though it may not be visible.

6. I will give unto him that is athirst. Nothing will be
grudged to those who ask. Life in all its fulness of energy and
beauty is offered and one day the hidden fulfilment will be
outwardly realized.

7. He that overcometh. Christ here reminds the Seer what
He has said so often before (see cc. ii., iii.) that great and
wonderful as are the blessings of the new life they are only given
to the victors. The holy city is made up of those who have
conquered. It is this which makes certain the relationship
between God and His children. They are not only His by
creation and the mystic adoption by Baptism, but also by the
moral union of similarity of aims. They have conquered as
Christ did.

8. But for the fearful etc. The first in this awful catalogue
are the "cowardly," those who prefer ease and self-indulgence to
the hardness of the Christian life, and next to them are placed
the faithless, those who by act or word have denied the faith.
The abominable are those tainted with heathen abominations,
those guilty of monstrous sins.

and all liars, their part *shall be* in the lake that burneth with fire and brimstone ; which is the second death.

XXI. 9-27.   *The Vision of the New Jerusalem.*

And there came one of the seven angels who had the 9 seven bowls, who were laden with the seven last plagues ; and he spake with me, saying, Come hither, I will shew thee the bride, the wife of the Lamb. And he carried me away 10 in the Spirit to a mountain great and high, and shewed me the holy city Jerusalem, coming down out of heaven from God, having the glory of God : her light was like 11 unto a stone most precious, as it were a jasper stone, clear as crystal : having a wall great and high ; having twelve 12 gates, and at the gates twelve angels ; and names written

---

9. 10.   Come hither, I will shew thee.   When the Seer was shewn Babylon, he was taken into the desert ; but when Jerusalem, the angel takes him to a great and lofty mountain.   We must mount up "on eagle's wings" if we are to see God's Ideals.

10.   coming down out of heaven.   The Church is of heaven not of earth and all the beauty she possesses is of God, she has none of her own.

11.   her light.   Two words are used for light—one for what it is absolutely, the other for what it is in its derived character. See Gen. i., God said "Let there be light...," and He made two luminaries, i.e. two means or instruments by which the light could be conveyed.   So the Church has no light except that which she obtains from the Light of the World.

The jasper here to which her light is compared was probably something like a diamond.

12.   a wall great and high.   The wall encompassed the city and was very high as we judge height, namely 216 feet, but low compared with the height of the city which was over 1300 miles. It shone with great brilliancy and it was cased with jasper, and was built on twelve huge blocks each adorned with precious stones.   By this wall is meant the Faith and Doctrine of Christ which is Apostolic, for its foundations are all marked with the names of the Apostles.   And this faith is a beautiful thing especially when adorned with the jewels of holy lives (see *vv.* 17 and 18).

twelve gates.   The gates are at varying intervals, three on

thereon, which are *the names* of the twelve tribes of the
13 children of Israel : on the east were three gates ; and on
the north three gates ; and on the south three gates ; and
14 on the west three gates. And the wall of the city had
twelve foundations, and on them twelve names of the
15 twelve apostles of the Lamb. And he that spake with me
had for a measure a golden reed to measure the city, and
16 the gates thereof, and the wall thereof. And the city lieth
foursquare, and the length thereof is as great as the
breadth : and he measured the city with the reed, twelve
thousand furlongs : the length and the breadth and the
17 height thereof are equal. And he measured the wall
thereof, a hundred and forty and four cubits, *according to*
18 the measure of a man, that is, of an angel. And the

---

each side of the city which lies foursquare. They were made
of pearl. The entrance into the Kingdom is through purity, and
no matter from what quarter an applicant comes, if he be holy
he is admitted. There are angels posted to prevent the entrance
of anything that is unclean. The number of gates testifies to the
great freedom of entrance, for they are always open, day and
night (see *v.* 25).

14. the wall of the city had twelve foundations. The
gates are marked with the names of the twelve tribes, because
through the Old Testament we approach the thought of the
New: but the strength of the city itself lies in the faith of the
Apostolic body. "No other foundation can any man lay than
that which is laid" (1 Cor. iii. 11). See also Matt. xvi. 8 and
1 Pet. ii. 6.

17. And he measured the wall. This is not a measurement
with a view to marking the city off apart, but of giving an
impression of spiritual proportion and size. It was a perfect
quadrilateral cube and each side measured 1500 miles. A city
the size of Russia with buildings rising miles and miles into
the clouds is that which we are to imagine if we slavishly follow
the figures given. St John's object is of course not material but
spiritual. It is to put into figures what St Paul puts into words
(Eph. iii. 18). Love which is the character of the city is
practically immeasurable and is as broad and deep as it is lofty.
Gold is the symbol of love and of this the city was made ; only
it was free from the coarseness of passion, the gold being bright
like clear glass.

building of the wall thereof was jasper : and the city was
pure gold, like unto pure glass.   The foundations of the 19
wall of the city were adorned with all manner of precious
stones.   The first foundation was jasper ; the second,
sapphire ; the third, chalcedony ; the fourth, emerald ; the 20
fifth, sardonyx ; the sixth, sardius ; the seventh, chrysolite ;
the eighth, beryl ; the ninth, topaz ; the tenth, chryso-
prase ; the eleventh, jacinth ; the twelfth, amethyst.
And the twelve gates were twelve pearls ; each one of the 21
several gates was of one pearl : and the street of the city
was pure gold, as it were transparent glass.   And I saw 22
no temple therein : for the Lord God the Almighty, and
the Lamb, are the temple thereof.   And the city hath 23
no need of the sun, neither of the moon, to shine upon it :

---

18. the building of the wall thereof was jasper. Jasper
(see iv. 2) symbolizes justice, and the bulwarks of the heavenly
city are the laws of righteousness which keep the city.

**19. The foundations of the wall of the city were adorned
with all manner of precious stones.** Note the added glory
and richness of the adornments of the city compared with the
glittering tinsel of the harlot's dress.   The beauty in store for
the Christian is far more attractive and glorious than that which
the world has to offer.   "The foundation stones represent the
fundamental principles on which God's City is built : as twelve
they indicate their numerical completeness ; as shining with a
common lustre their unity ; as stones of different hues their
manifoldness, as brilliant stones the glorification of this earthly
life through the light of heaven" (Lange).

21. And the twelve gates were twelve pearls. Though the
underlying principles of Christianity are so different, St Paul,
St Peter, St James, St John, etc. all expressing various gifts, the
gates are all the same.   The pearl here may stand for truth or
for purity, for it is equally true that no man enters except
through Christ the Truth, and that without holiness no man
shall see the Lord.

22. I saw no temple. "The city possesses no sanctuary, for
it is itself a Holy of Holies, as its cubic form suggests" (Swete).
See 2 Cor. vi. 16.

the Lord God the Almighty and the Lamb. The association of
these names is most significant and could only have been placed
by one who recognised the Deity of Christ.   The Divine Presence
is expressed as it were in a double way.

for the glory of God did lighten it, and the lamp thereof
24 *is* the Lamb. And the nations shall walk amidst the light
thereof : and the kings of the earth do bring their glory
25 into it. And the gates thereof shall in no wise be shut by
26 day (for there shall be no night there) : and they shall
bring the glory and the honour of the nations into it :
27 and there shall in no wise enter into it anything unclean,
or he that maketh an abomination and a lie : but only
22 they which are written in the Lamb's book of life. And
he shewed me a river of water of life, bright as crystal,
proceeding out of the throne of God and of the Lamb,

---

23. the glory of God did lighten it. No created light is
necessary in the Holy City, for the full beauty and splendour of
God shines there without any intercepting medium such as we
know here.

24. And the nations shall walk. Partially fulfilled now,
when all nations, heathen as well as Christian, gain high advan-
tages through the Church. Its complete fulfilment would seem
to indicate that in the future beyond the grave national life will
still be preserved. A further thought given is the contribution
that each nation will make to the beauty and glory of the city.

25. there shall be no night there. "In the history of
nations as in nature, darkness succeeds to light, civilization is
followed by outbursts of barbarism. In the ideal Church no
such relapses are possible ; the future holds no dark ages for the
City of God" (Swete).

See Jn. x. 9 and for a contrast Matt. xxv. 10.

27. there shall in no wise enter into it anything unclean.
This feature is the great attraction to all who long for a perfect
society. In the City no one is common (see mg.), everyone is
distinguished and nothing is heard or seen that could shock the
most sensitive conscience.

XXII. 1. And he shewed me a river of water of life.
See Ezek. xlvii. 1-12 and Gen. ii. 9 : and note the differences in
the description here. The river flows from the Throne through
the middle of the City and on its banks are trees which bear
twelve varieties of fruit in the year and wonderful leaves which
heal the nations.

This river is an image of the Holy Spirit the Giver of Life
Who proceeds from the Father and the Son and through His
action on human nature produces such wonderful fruits as we
read of in Gal. **v. 22,** and also graces which purify national life.

in the midst of the street thereof. And on this side of 2
the river and on that was the tree of life, bearing twelve
manner of fruits, yielding its fruit every month : and the
leaves of the tree were for the healing of the nations.
And there shall be no curse any more : and the throne of 3
God and of the Lamb shall be therein : and his servants
shall do him service ; and they shall see his face ; and his 4
name *shall be* on their foreheads. And there shall be 5
night no more ; and they need no light of lamp, neither
light of sun ; for the Lord God shall give them light :
and they shall reign for ever and ever.

PART IX. EPILOGUE. LAST WORDS OF THE ANGEL, THE SEER AND THE LORD.

XXII. 6-20. *Conclusion.*

The second volume ends at *v.* 5, but the author adds these
  fifteen verses as testimony to the value and importance
  of the Truth which the Revelation of the Lord has made
  known. First, an Angel bears witness to it and to the
  great advantage that belongs to those who remember it. It
  is not therefore to be laid by, as though it had only relation
  to the last things. Then follows the testimony of Christ
  and lastly that of the Apostle specially addressed to those
  who might tamper with it.

And he said unto me, These words are faithful and 6
true : and the Lord, the God of the spirits of the prophets,

---

3. and the throne of God and of the Lamb. The great
blessing of the Heavenly City is the Presence of God and Christ
—visible in some inconceivable way and shining in the intelligence of all His servants.

5. And there shall be night no more. The darkness and
uncertainty of life as we know it will be gone. We shall see
the meaning of life and need no explanation whether through the
Bible or the Church. And the dominion man was created to
exercise will be his through the ages. The saints are reigning
now (xx. 4), but after the completion of this age their reign will
be manifested.

6. These words are faithful. The "sayings" of the whole
prophecy are so wonderful that the angel confirms their testimony.

sent his angel to shew unto his servants the things which
7 must shortly come to pass. And behold, I come quickly.
Blessed is he that keepeth the words of the prophecy of
this book.

8 And I John am he that heard and saw these things.
And when I heard and saw, I fell down to worship
before the feet of the angel which shewed me these things.
9 And he saith unto me, See thou do it not : I am a fellow-
servant with thee and with thy brethren the prophets, and
with them which keep the words of this book : worship
God.

10 And he saith unto me, Seal not up the words of the
11 prophecy of this book ; for the time is at hand. He that
is unrighteous, let him do unrighteousness still : and he
that is filthy, let him be made filthy still : and he that is
righteous, let him do righteousness still : and he that is
12 holy, let him be made holy still. Behold, I come quickly ;
and my reward is with me, to render to each man accord-
13 ing as his work is. I am the Alpha and the Omega, the

They are to be relied upon, he says, for they come through
the inspiration of God Himself and will soon be realized, for the
Lord is coming very soon.

8. And I John am he that heard and saw. This last vision
caused the Apostle to forget the warning he had already received
and to worship the angel who shewed him the vision. But again
he was forbidden on the ground that the angel was his fellow-
servant in the great company of God.

10. Seal not up the words. See Dan. viii. 26 where the
opposite counsel is given. The prophecy in spite of the
strange mysteries it contains is not to be kept secret but to be
read and pondered over, because the time of its fulfilment is
close at hand. The Fall of Rome was not far distant and the
Church ought to be prepared for the change.

11. He that is unrighteous. See Dan. xii. 10. The second
coming of the Lord whenever it happens will have the effect of
confirming the dispositions of people. There will be no change
then—the bad will remain bad and the good will remain good
(Matt. xxv. 10).

12. my reward is with me. Everyone will have such
prizes as he deserved (see Ps. lxi. 13; Job xxxiv. 11; Ps. xl. 14;

first and the last, the beginning and the end. Blessed 14
are they that wash their robes, that they may have the
right *to come* to the tree of life, and may enter in by
the gates into the city. Without are the dogs, and the 15
sorcerers, and the fornicators, and the murderers, and
the idolaters, and every one that loveth and maketh a lie.

I Jesus have sent mine angel to testify unto you these 16
things for the churches. I am the root and the offspring
of David, the bright, the morning star.

And the Spirit and the bride say, Come. And he that 17
heareth, let him say, Come. And he that is athirst, let
him come : he that will, let him take the water of life
freely.

I testify unto every man that heareth the words of the 18
prophecy of this book, If any man shall add unto them,

Rev. ii. 23), and receive them at His Hands Who sums up all
life, Who is its Beginning and its Ending.

14. Blessed are they that wash their robes. Though man
is rewarded for his work, his work is very full of stains and needs
to be plunged into the Incarnate Life of Christ and to be washed.
Only those who have clean garments are allowed admission to
the Tree of Life. For no unclean person has any place in the
fair city. See our Lord's Parable of the Marriage Garment.

15. Without are the dogs. To the Eastern, the dog had no
attractions. He was the scavenger of the streets without home
or owner and here depicts the greedy selfish wandering soul.
See Ps. lix. 6, 14, 15 and 1 K. xiv. 11; Mk. vii. 27.
Witchcraft, impurity, violence and idolatry have no place in the
city. Note here and in xxi. 27 St John's hatred of lying. How
impossible that one who was not true himself should write such
words!

16. I Jesus have sent. This is the guarantee of the truth of
the book which would necessarily excite so much questioning.
It has the certificate of One who is the Beginning and End of
the human race and its one Hope.

17. And the Spirit and the bride. The Church from within
and from without, i.e. in its inner spirit and outward devotion,
cry out for the coming of Christ, and the hope the author
expresses is that everyone who reads his book may be filled with
the same great desire.

18, 19. I testify unto every man that heareth etc. A

God shall add unto him the plagues which are written in
19 this book : and if any man shall take away from the
words of the book of this prophecy, God shall take away
his part from the tree of life, and out of the holy city,
which are written in this book.

20   He which testifieth these things saith, Yea : I come
quickly.   Amen : come, Lord Jesus.

21   The grace of the Lord Jesus be with the saints.   Amen.

---

solemn warning against any who would dare to alter by ad-
dition or omission the prophecy of the book.

20. Yea: I come quickly.   The words were written nearly
2000 years ago and at first excite in us some surprise.   But
Christ's comings are not confined to the last great coming.   He
comes in every great critical period of history, such as the
destruction of Jerusalem, and brings the end sensibly nearer.

INDEX

For EU product safety concerns, contact us at Calle de José Abascal, 56–1°,
28003 Madrid, Spain or eugpsr@cambridge.org.

www.ingramcontent.com/pod-product-compliance
Ingram Content Group UK Ltd.
Pitfield, Milton Keynes, MK11 3LW, UK
UKHW020312140625
459647UK00018B/1835